Introduction to

AFRICAN ARTS

of Kenya, Zaire, and Nigeria

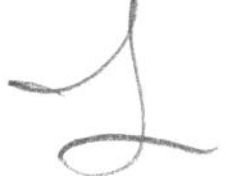

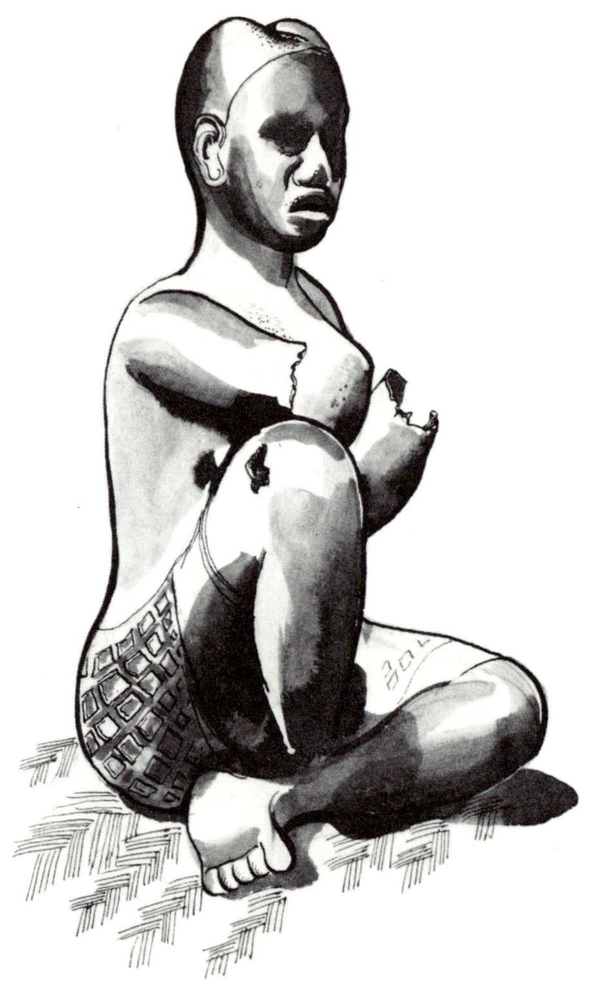

Fig. 1. Seated bronze figure at Tada, Ife School. Bronze over clay. Height approximately 20 inches. *circa* 13/14 century. Middle Niger. One of six figures kept *in situ* by the Federal Nigerian Department of Antiquities. Note the hands and feet worn away by ritual scrubbing.

Introduction to
AFRICAN ARTS

of Kenya, Zaire, and Nigeria

by Fred J. Parrott

ILLUSTRATIONS BY NAOMICHI KIMURA

ARCO PUBLISHING COMPANY, INC.
219 Park Avenue South, New York, N.Y. 10003

Published by Arco Publishing Company, Inc.
219 Park Avenue South, New York, N.Y.

Copyright © 1972 by Fred J. Parrott
All rights reserved

Library of Congress Catalog Card Number 72-3332
Paperback: ISBN 0-668-02668-5
Library Binding: ISBN 0-668-02669-3

Printed in United States of America

ACKNOWLEDGMENTS

With appreciation to Dr. Benjamin L. Perry, Jr., President of Florida A and M University, for encouragement and assistance and to Dr. Leedell W. Neyland, Dean of Arts and Sciences, and his office staff; to Florida A and M University Research Committee for a grant under Institutional Research, to the Department of Sociology and to the Coleman Library Staff.

Special thanks are due to many friends and colleagues for advice and assistance and in particular Eva May Atwood of the Florida State University faculty, Emory T. Trosper, Jr., University of Maryland, Leslie N. Wilson, William E. H. Howard, and James Mitchell of the Florida A and M faculty, Moses Ihonde of the Consulate General of Nigeria, Charles Chikeka and E. Babafimi Campbell of Nigeria, Henry Olela of Kenya, Manuel F. Domingos of Zaire and generally my students at Florida A and M University for whom this and a preliminary study *The Wind in a Sieve* were originally prepared.

The sketches were drawn by Naomichi Kimura at the American Cultural Centre, Tokyo, Japan.

Foreword

This survey of African art is intended to stimulate further study and investigation. Its general objective is to foster appreciation and understanding of the contemporary African renaissance and to stress the concept that African art, like all artistic expression, is essentially ambivalent—both unique and universal, revealing man's identity as an individual and also his status as a human being.

The African artist, like artists everywhere in whatever time or place or culture, searches for personal freedom. He seeks to embellish and to record an experience, to establish and to communicate an identity which will not only describe himself as an individual but also at the same time link him to others.

This central focus is contained in the statement by Ayo Ogunshaye quoted in full context in the Concluding Comment: "In the world of culture we are all builders, all borrowers and lenders." The statement supports two basic contentions: first, man's identity may be revealed by what he produces artistically, and second, man can preserve a portion of his identity through an interchange of his artistic production and at the same time promote unity and understanding among peoples.

To discover and appreciate some portions of the artistic expression in Africa as well as western and eastern cultures may help strengthen the concept of the Community of Man, confirming his uniqueness as an individual and his universality as a member of the human race.

The contemporary African artistic renaissance, popularized by the sweeping acceptance of Afro styles and undergirded by explosive evidence of Black Power, seeks to reaffirm an African identity. The nature of this identity arouses curiosity and concern and confusion.

There is curiosity because less than two decades ago Africa to most North Americans was remote and dark and alien, a place of turmoil, full of jungles and wild animals, unpleasantly tropical and peopled by natives with leanings toward headhunting and cannibalism. It has been a continent grossly exploited by foreign traders and frequently proselytized by missionaries both Christian and Moslem, where white European marauders (and also a quite considerable number of darker skinned Arabians and native black Africans) conducted incredible traffic in human slavery.

There is concern because some black North Americans struggling for recognition after generations of repression and insecurity consider Africa a kind of romantic homeland, held heart-close at times in dreams but somehow also remote and vague, where grew the roots of their identity. Yet, tragically, some black Americans who have travelled to Africa seeking that identity and the fulfillment of that dream have discovered themselves strangers in Africa, more alien than they were on this western continent, which is their birthplace and their environment, although they have more frequently than not abided on the fringes of the white man's world. Some have discovered that their black brothers in Africa do not accept them merely because their skin is also black. The black Africans sometimes resent them because of their seemingly arrogant western ways. Like many another western traveler, black Americans visiting Africa have found themselves tourists and outsiders.

And there is confusion because the black African native in the midst of resurgence and renaissance finds himself presently confronted with massive conflicts. Although his primary objective may be the early liquidation of colonialism and racism and the establishment of an African personality based upon African achievements worthy of recognition in the world community, his direction is uncertain. He seeks to reimpose a native culture upon a society disoriented by the white man's infiltration, or at least to synthesize the indigenous with the foreign, the ancient with the modern.

When Langston Hughes collected and published *An African Treasury* of native African prose many years ago, the term "negritude" predominated to describe the purely African. Perhaps the term may still serve to describe that sense of togetherness or identity which might conceivably characterize the black African culture. Among black Africans themselves, focus upon "negritude" reflects their attempt to rediscover a native African personality.

But so vast and so complex and so lacking in unity is the continent of Africa, even within the more specific areas of Kenya, the Republic of Zaire (formerly the Democratic Republic of Congo), and Nigeria, that nothing may be termed precisely typical. No "characteristic" can be singled out without considerable distortion or oversimplification of truth. In countries so regionally varied—with differences in terrain and of foreign influence, with a multiplicity of languages so distinct and separate from each other that one group within an area cannot communicate with another group in the same area, with divergent traditional tribal customs—arts and crafts have not usually been interchangeable.

A considerable portion of what the westerner might call "African disunity" may be explained by the African concept of tribal loyalties. ("Tribe"by dictionary definition is any aggregate of people united by ties of descent from a common ancestor which results in a community of customs and traditions.) African society traditionally consists of many separate family or lineage groups; the family takes precedence and is considered more significant than any larger social or political group or the authority of any individual ruler. Ancestor worship in

African religion expresses veneration for the family; power or energy from the ancestral god may be transferred to the fetish object or to the mask and become symbolic of the power of the tribe. The basis of African religion is energy and not matter; and the energy may be a tribal concern.

Jomo Kenyatta, in *Facing Mount Kenya,* concludes:

The key to this culture is the tribal system, and the bases of the tribal system are the family group and the age-grades, which between them shape the character and determine the outlook of every man, woman, and child in Gikuyu society. According to Gikuyu ways of thinking, nobody is an isolated individual. Or rather, his uniqueness is a secondary fact about him: first and foremost he is several people's relative and several people's contemporary. His life is founded on this fact spiritually and economically, just as much as biologically; the work he does every day is determined by it, and it is the basis of his sense of moral responsibility and social obligation. His personal needs, physical and psychological, are satisfied incidentally while he plays his part as member of a family group, and cannot be fully satisfied in any other way. The fact that in Gikuyu language individualism is associated with black magic, and that a man or woman is honoured by being addressed as somebody's parent, or somebody's uncle or aunt, shows how indispensably kinship is at the root of the Gikuyu idea of good and evil.(1)

And G. T. Basden, in his book *Among the Ibos of Nigeria,* has this to say about the significance of the tribe:

The will of the tribe or family, expressed or implied, permeates his whole being, and is the deciding factor in every detail of his life. It is a sort of intangible freemasonry; the essence of the primary instincts of the people. Men constantly act contrary to their better judgment, and, at times, even wrongly, because they firmly believe they have no alternative: they dare not oppose the wishes of their people. Consequently though there may be independent thought, there is seldom independent action, probably never where other members of the tribe or family are involved, however remotely. A further result, and one which must always be borne in mind by the foreign inquirer into primitive customs, is that the ideas of the native are indefinite. He has no fixed thoughts. He is under the influence of an atmosphere which emanates from the whole tribe. This subliminal consciousness, by which all his movements are controlled, becomes practically a sixth sense. It is inexpressible in words but, nevertheless, extremely powerful in action.(2)

So all-pervading is the tradition of the tribal or group effort that constructing a boat or decorating it may become a communal affair: the pattern may be set perhaps by a skilled individual but many hands work it out, each adding his own detail. An expert in sculpture may serve several tribes as a kind of sanctified or inspired individual and to him several families may send a potentially skilled member to study as a kind of apprentice.

Distinctness and separateness of various tribal groups, on the other hand, because of so many specific and differing tribal loyalties, may impede the development of a national culture or national state. Only very recently instituted, African nationalism attempts to follow the pattern of an alien western culture. Because of the traditional concept of tribal loyalties, it may be difficult for many black Africans to accept a western concept of precisely determinate law and a government which supercedes and supplants the family.

Perhaps a proper negritude persists just beneath the surface in Africa. Perhaps there are common roots and beliefs, myths and traditions, which could be considered characteristic. But in a comparative examination they might also turn out to be astonishingly more simiilar to the cultural heritage of the East or West than different from it. "Too much has been written," says Professor Wingert, "about the 'magical' and 'strange' qualities to be found in this art, and too little attention has been paid to the fact that the needs, aspirations, and longings of mankind are similar whether one is considering primitive peoples or the peoples of the Gothic Age in western Europe." (3) The varied artistic expression of these African countries reveals surprising similarities with that of other races in other times and places.

In all primitive societies, for instance, consciousness of something outside oneself finds expression in animistic beliefs and the attempt to depict the spiritual essence as well as a physical likeness in a carving or a drawing. The artist creates abstractions which distort or mold materials into a form more idealised than realistic. He learns his craft by observation and practice under the instruction of an elder craftsman, and he tends to perpetuate traditional styles and techniques. Artists everywhere have made use of materials close at hand. The sounds of birds and insects or animals may be imitated vocally to describe a condition or to evoke a mood and then later be refined and elaborated into patterns of music. In Africa, as elsewhere, primitive man not only provided himself with food and shelter but somehow managed to make his diet more palatable by learning to cook and to make his shelter more attractive by adding decoration.

This introductory survey of African art describes samplings from the arts and the conditions which surrounded their production in three African countries south of the Sahara: Kenya in the east, the Republic of Zaire in the center, and Nigeria in the west. The samplings include items of general information and a brief sketch of the history and the current condition of places and peoples and things, but the focus centers upon artistic expression.

Essentially chronological and regional, the survey attempts to discuss artistic expression in these countries during three different eras: Traditional—the ancient, primitive, pre-literate heritage; Colonial—the period of foreign occupation; and Contemporary—the modern search for identity and synthesis.

Contents

Introduction to

AFRICAN ARTS

of Kenya, Zaire, and Nigeria

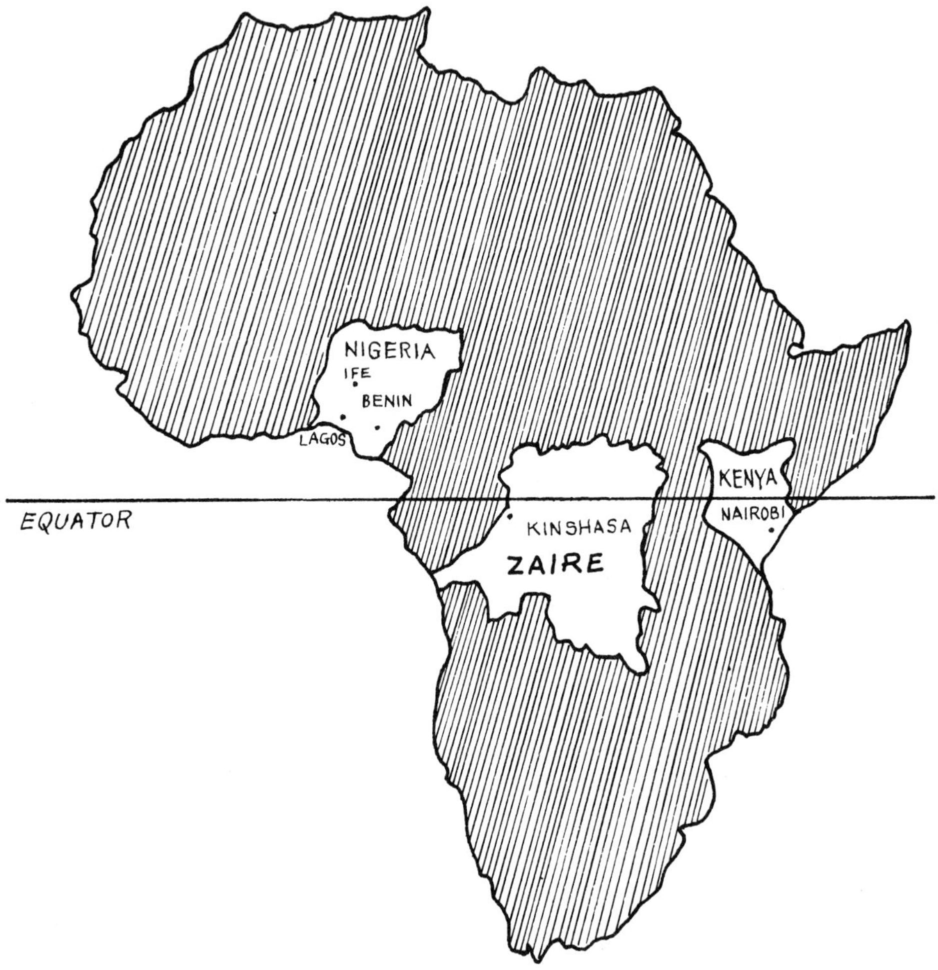

Fig. 2. *Map of Africa*—showing relative locations of Nigeria, the Republic of Zaire, and Kenya.

General Information

Fourteen hundred years before Pericles and the Golden Age of Greece, Nok culture existed in northern Nigeria. Today, museums exhibit terra-cotta figurines from that ancient culture; they are curiously abstract and yet artistically and distinctively expressive.

By the fourth century, or about the height of the Roman Empire, which purportedly disintegrated around A.D. 410, great states were established in Africa in the eastern area of the Sudan; and by the eleventh century the Ghana Empire had been infiltrated from North Africa by the Muslims. Eventually this Empire gave rise to the Afro-Muslim Kingdom of Mali extending over fifteen hundred miles. Later, under the rule of the Negroid-Mandingoes (Islam converts), the fabulous metropolis of Timbuktu boasted a great Mosque and a university for the study of the Koran and the statistic that twelve thousand caravans visited the city. (1)

Complexity of origin, complexity of foreign interpenetration, complexity and profusion of languages (most of them verbal only), and complexity of religions befuddle any attempt to categorize or to classify or to analyze African artistic production. Only fairly recently has any very considerable systematic study been made of the art of Africa. As yet much of the background and the philosophy and the tradition which gave rise to the artistic expression in Africa is unknown.

But from the samplings studied thus far, it is increasingly evident that this vast region produced and may continue to produce an art as impressive as that of any great western or eastern civilization.

African ethnic beginnings no man can ever know for certain. The original African ethnic group may have been an indigenous and very ancient race—an "autochthonic" people—called "Nigrillo" (a people who were dark-skinned and small in stature, perhaps similar to the Pygmies or the Bushmen of central Zaire).(2) The Nigrillos, submerged by waves of immigrants from the south and east, eventually mingled with invaders from the Near East and Asia, who came from the north and the east, and with Europeans, who came from the west.

Historically it would be difficult, if not impossible, to establish the identity which is purely African. Martin Lasky speculates upon this in his traveler's notebook, called *Africa for Beginners,* when considering the problem of African identity in contemporary Nigeria. "What is a real sense of identity?" he writes. "In Lagos the most exclusive association by far is the so-called 'Brazilian Club' and the membership consists only of the descendents of Latin America's African slaves! . . . Will change strike a balance with continuity? . . . especially here where (yesterday) the grandson of a village rainmaker becomes director of the new meteorological institute. . . ."

Geographically the African continent offers surprises for those who are unfamiliar with its topographical features and its population.

The continent of Africa is crossed just below its center by the equator, but the climate ranges from tropical to temperate owing to variation in terrain. On the high plateaus and in the mountainous areas along the equator African temperature can be more chilly than hot. Less than ten per cent of Africa is jungle. All but a very inconsiderable portion of the land has been explored.

Africa is nearly three times the size of continental United States of America—exceeding this country in area by nearly eight million square miles.(3) And Africa has approximately 130 million more people than the United States.

In 1972 there existed in continental Africa forty-three independent countries and four countries under foreign control, plus various island territories still under foreign domination.*

KENYA

Kenya, which lies astride the equator in east Africa, is approximately the size of New Mexico and only slightly smaller than Texas. It abounds with wild life. So-called "bush areas"—which really aren't bush at all but large flat arid plains covered with rough stubble and dotted with thorn trees and clumps of high grass—resemble an enormous public zoo. The bush attracts tourists the world over who come on "safari" (the Swahili word for "trip" or "journey"). Tourists come now as frequently with cameras to take pictures as formerly they came with guns to shoot and kill. And the tourists go bouncing over the rough terrain in sturdy jeeps driven by native guides—while lions and antelope and vultures and wildebeest (also known as "gnu") and giraffes and elephants continue on about their business more or less unperturbed by this intrusion. Most of the bush area is protected and controlled as a game preserve by the government.

Much of Kenya is tropical and hot but much of it is not. Ranging from a low coastal plain to a high plateau some 10,000 feet above sea level with a semi-desert in the north, it has astonishing topographical and climatic variety. Snow covers Mt. Kenya continuously.

Of the ten million inhabitants of Kenya—roughly comparable to the population of Ohio—97 per cent are African and mix-blooded Somali, the largest ethnic group being the Bantu Kikuyu. Approximately 60 per cent are Christian and 3 per cent Muslim.

---

* According to the research of Dr. William E. H. Howard, Professor of Political Science at Florida A and M University.

Swahali and English are the official languages, but hundreds of native dialects are spoken.

The capital city of Nairobi is lined with ultra-modern buildings. It compares in population with Norfolk, Virginia, or Omaha, Nebraska, with nearly 300,000 people.

Sailors and traders have visited Kenya since the Middle Ages via the Indian Ocean from Asia and Arabia. Many trading posts were established early in Kenya's history. The Portuguese arrived in 1498 and stayed two centuries until driven out by the Arabs. And then the British took over. During these years trading in ivory and slaves was the chief attraction. In 1895 Kenya became a British Protectorate, and the British built a railroad across the country to Lake Victoria. Englishmen and white South Africans settled there in great numbers. After this came the horrendous Mau Mau uprising—probably sparked by Jomo Kenyata, the nationalist leader of the Kikuyu radicals: 12,000 were killed (but only thirty-five Europeans!) and 80,000 imprisoned.(4) Thereafter the British negotiated a new constitution and in 1962 Kenyatta became the first president. As recently as 1967, constitutional changes established a single National Assembly. Kenya is an independent republic in the Commonwealth of Nations. Recently, conflict among various political factions within the government has caused turbulence and strife, but in 1972 Jomo Kenyatta, the aging national leader, remained head of state and in control of the executive administration.

THE DEMOCRATIC REPUBLIC OF ZAIRE

The third largest nation in Africa, almost six times the size of California, is the Democratic Republic of Zaire (formerly Congo-Kinshasa) with its capital at Kinshasa, formerly Leopoldville—a city about the size of Cincinnati or Baltimore. The Congo River snakes across the middle of the country, dividing it almost precisely in half. It is one of the largest rivers in the world. Dense forest covers much of Zaire with terrain which is frequently swampy and always humid, except in the mountains and high plateaus. Although generally the climate is tropical, temperate zones exist in the west and in the south. Elephants, lions, gorillas, hippopotami, crocodiles, pythons and other wild life abound. Zaire produces 8 per cent of the world's copper and boasts the largest amounts of cobalt and industrial diamonds in the world.(5)

Until June 30, 1960 and the establishment of the presidential regime under the controversial national hero, Patrice Lumumba, Belgian jurisdiction dominated. A long and turbulant history preceded the era in which King Leopold II of Belgium took it upon himself to initiate exploration of the country—eventually establishing the so-called "Congo Free State" with himself as King. British exploratory expeditions under Livingston and Stanley followed, and a long stormy period of secessions and rebellion until the 1960 independence. Today, a tightly organized Zairien National Army assures the "security and the territorial integrity of the Democratic Republic."(6)

In August 1971, the President, Lieutenant-General Joseph Desire Mobutu, changed the name of the country from the Democratic Republic of Congo to the Democratic Republic of Zaire. President Mobutu believed that the name Congo (from the Mukongo tribe) did not truly represent all component groups in the country. He renamed the country Zaire, after the original name of the river which flows through the country.

There are eight administrative provinces in Zaire in addition to the capitol at Kinshasa. The population of Zaire has four major ethnic groups—Pygmies (comparatively few), Bantus (about eight or nine million constituting the great mass of the population), the Soudanese, and the Nilotics. Almost every ethnic group has a multitude of local dialects; it is said that the Bantu dialects alone number more than two hundred. But five major languages in addition to English predominate: Swahili, Tshilumba, Kikongo, Lingala, and Lomongo.

One finds both Protestant and Catholic churches in Zaire (Chris-

tian missionaries having been present early and for long) as well as native Kimbanguist churches following the precepts of the Prophet Si-
mon Kimbangu of the Lower Congo. Also there are a number of
Islamic mosques.

The Republic of Zaire supports three Universities and some ten
institutions of higher education, including the National School of
Mines, the Medical Training Institute, and the Advanced Institute of
Art and Architecture and Academy of Fine Arts, where the aim is the
training of artists in the fields of painting, sculpture, ceramics and
architecture.

NIGERIA

Sometimes called "land of the mighty river" or "country of great
waters" because of the Niger River from which it gets its name, Nigeria is the world's most populous Negro nation, presently comprising
some sixty million people or about one-fifth of the population of the
African continent. There exist some 250 tribal or linguistic groups in
this area of Africa, which is larger than Texas and Oklahoma combined.
Nigeria must by all counts be described in superlatives.

Two illustrations may suffice to support this conclusion:

First, Nigeria is most ancient in cultural and artistic heritage. The
oldest artifacts of African civilization, perhaps over two thousand years
old, were discovered in the Bauchi plateau in Northern Nigeria; others
very similar in the southwest near Ife are thought to be at least a thousand years old.(7) According to the myths of the Yoruba peoples, Ife
was the location of the origin of the earth. This is where the Supreme
Being (Ol-Orun) sent the Great God (Orish Nla) as his deputy with
a snail shell filled with sand to pour upon the marshy waters and a
pigeon and a five-toed chicken to spread the sand about until the sacred
chameleon could report the place sufficiently wide (the word "Ife"
means "wide") and dry for the creation of man. Later the Supreme
Being fashioned man out of the sacred earth of Ife.

Second, Nigeria may be one of the most turbulent and controversial of the independent African states owing to prolonged conflict resulting from civil war.

Although Nigeria is wholly within the tropics, the climate varies from the typically tropic along the coast to the subtropic inland. A great plateau of semi-desert land stretches across the northern part of the country, averaging 2,000 feet above sea level. The coastline covers more than five hundred miles with several important harbors of which Lagos—also the capital city—is one.

The tropical rainforest lies inland. Two rivers—the Niger and the Benue—have juncture at Lokoja, almost exactly in the center of the country. These rivers in places are navigable only by native dug-out canoes—since they vary in depth from rainy to dry season as much as thirty-five feet.

Nigeria is rich in natural resources—oil, coal, iron, tin, limestone, natural gas, and 48 per cent of the world's columbite (a product used in steel alloys). Tobacco, lumber, peanuts, skins, and great quantities of palm oil are also exported.

In the north the old Arabic caravan route brought the Islamic religion and culture to Nigeria, and Christian missionaries were ubiquitously present in the south. Yet the southern Yoruba tribes traditionally worshipped hundreds of different gods, each with special festival days and with traditional myths and legends, different rituals and distinctive ceremonial masks and other symbols.

For generations slave traders did profitable business in Nigeria. Arabian marauders from the north swept across the desert caravan routes and Europeans infiltrated from the western coastal areas into the interior.

The Obas, or chiefs, of the Benin tribes of the midwest dominated the area by virtue of the supremacy of their military might for many years. Like the Romans, the Benins conquered but they also ruled efficiently and they frequently adapted and absorbed the culture of those they dominated. Traditionally the Benin Obas were not only powerful but fabulously wealthy. They sent envoys as ambassadors to

Portugal—royal representatives gorgeously garbed and marvelously equipped with gifts and tokens. Legend has it that the spoon, previously unknown in Europe, was originally imported from Nigeria by the Benin Oba's envoy!

The Portuguese named Lagos; later the British administered it for nearly a century until it became the capital of a sovereign country in 1960, and, in 1963, capital of the First Republic of Nigeria under the British Commonwealth.

The First Republic of Nigeria (1963-1966), by somewhat arbitrary geographical division, comprised four districts, each with separate regional administrations: the Northern, the Western, the Eastern, and the Midwestern. All of these were under the central governmental administration of the Territory of Lagos—with a President as executive head and a two-house parliament.

In 1966 two successive military coups ushered in a period of strife complicated by profound cultural differences among the three predominating groups—the Hausa, the Yoruba, and the Ibo. The Second Republic of Nigeria was established with an administration controlled by the Federal Military Council and Major General Yakubu Gowon became Head of the Council and Commander-in-Chief of the Armed Forces. Following violent conflict, the Eastern Region seceded from Nigeria and proclaimed itself the separate autonomous Republic of Biafra with Colonel Odimegwu Ojukwa as Head of State. This resulted in a seemingly unresolvable civil war, and the conflict assumed international importance not alone because of the evidences of starvation and other cruelty suffered by civilians but also because of the evidence that the Russians and the British sided with the central Nigerian government and the French with the revolutionaries; the United States of America remained ostensibly neutral.

Eventually in 1970 the revolutionaries surrendered and the territorial integrity of Nigeria was restored under Gowon's military leadership.

Against this background of turbulence and confusion, Kenya, Zaire, and Nigeria emerged independent and self-governing after years of domination by foreign powers. An analysis of the artistic expression of these countries may lend a special perspective toward understanding and appreciating their cultures, for what man makes or fashions may reveal in large measure his identity; that which he is able to communicate effectively reflects not only his struggle toward personal freedom but also his impulse to share with others.

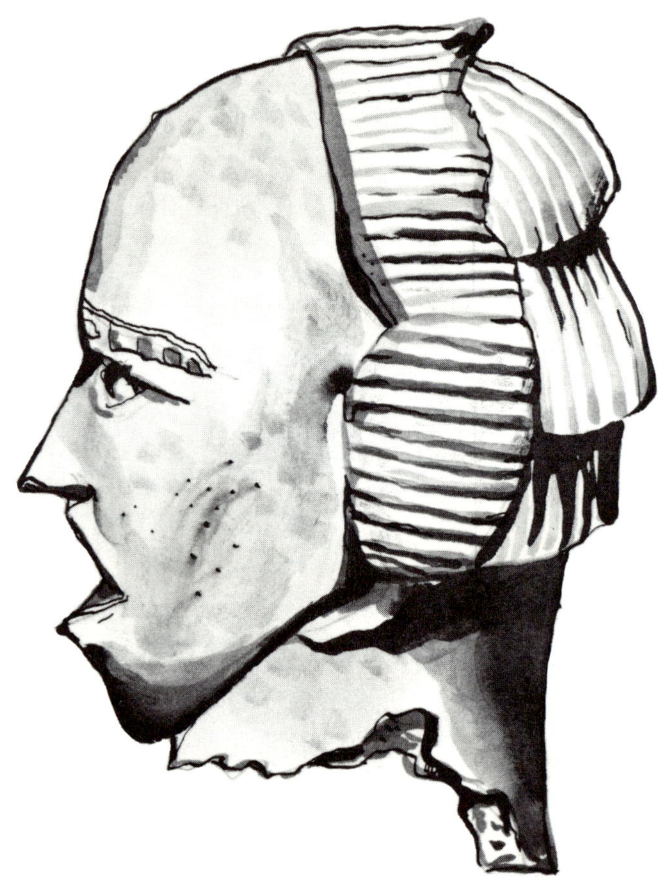

Fig. 3. Jema's Head (side view). Terra cotta. Approximately life-size. The Nok culture of northern Nigeria. Probably 2,000 years old.

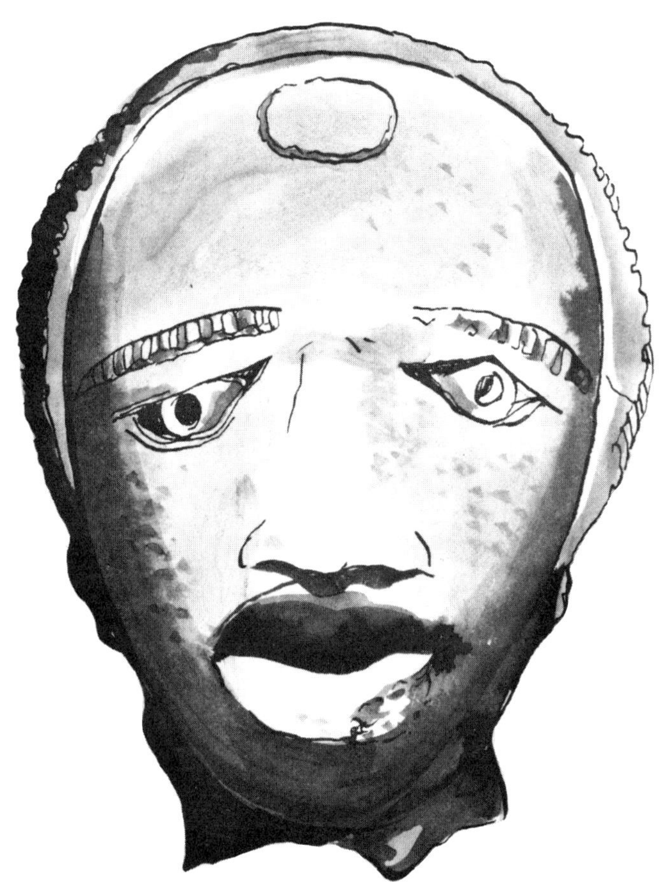

Fig. 4. Jema's Head (front view).

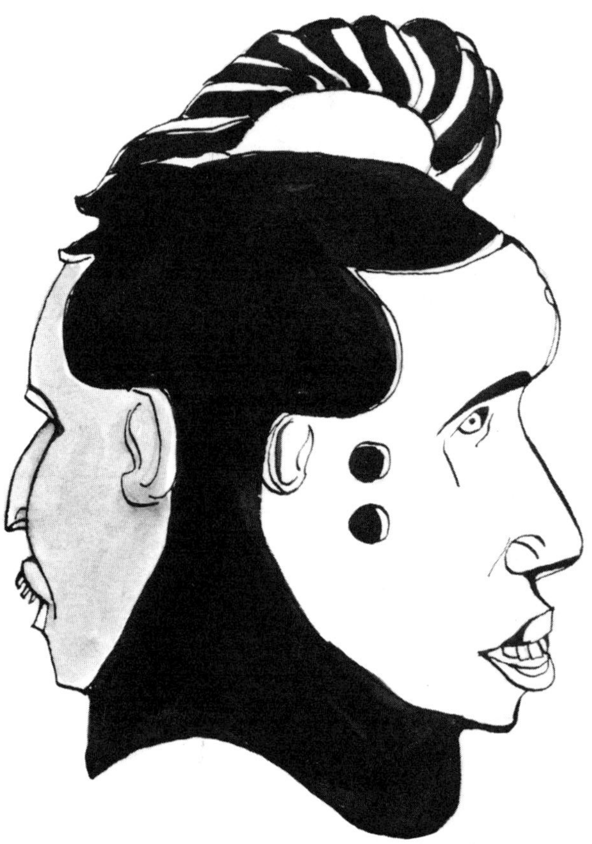

Fig. 5. Ekpo Ritual Mask. Skin-covered wood carving. Approximately life-size. Typical of the Ikoi of Nigeria; used in ancestor worshipping rites: symbol of the dead past and the living future. Of the two faces, one is male and black with closed eyes representing the past, the other face is female and white with open eyes representing the future. (Note the resemblance to the Janus figures of Roman household gods).

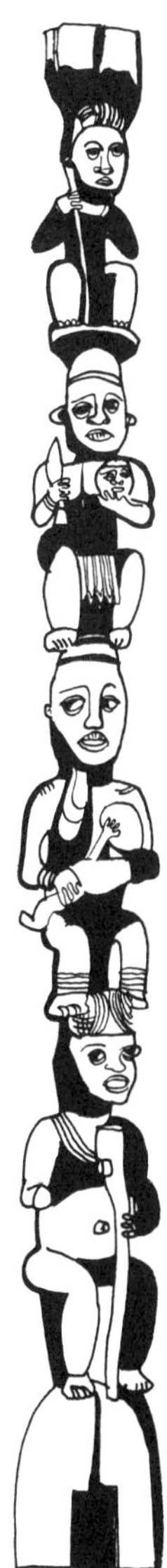

Fig. 6. House post. Wood-carved from a single tree trunk. Height approximately 10 fcct. Nigcria. The figures represent ancestors. (Note the resemblance to the totem poles of American Indians and Alaskans.)

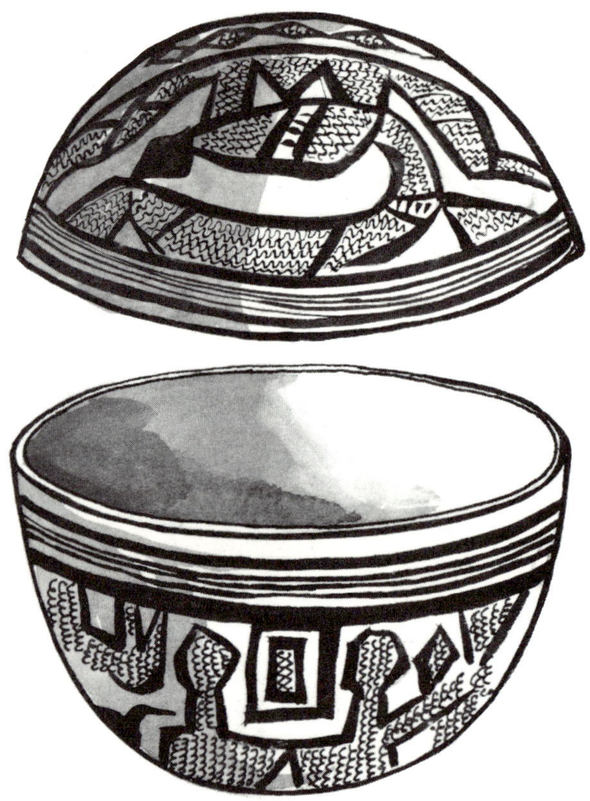

Fig. 7. Calabash. Vegetable gourd, carved and stained. Approximately 12 inches in diameter. Hausa of northern Nigeria. Used as a ceremonial vessel to receive temple offerings, and symbolizes heaven and earth: the top is the inverted bowl of the sky and the earth is below or floating inside like a small calabash in a larger one; the horizon is represented by the lip where the bowls join.

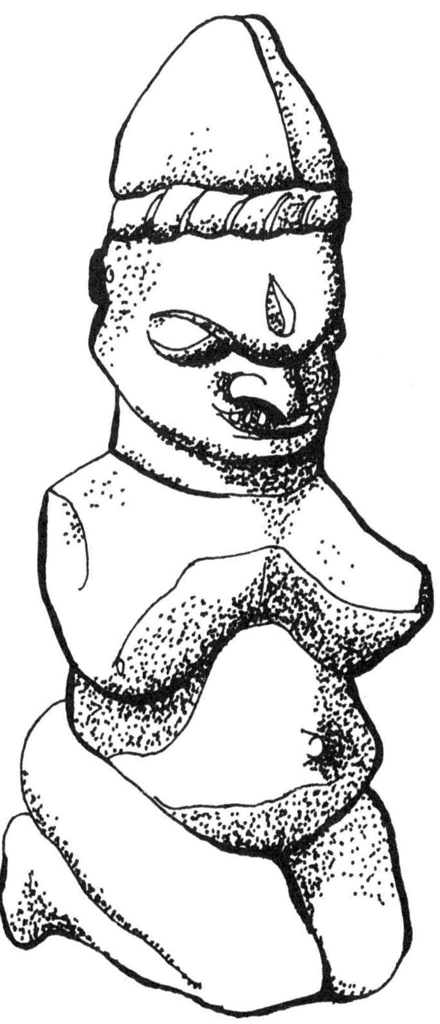

Fig. 8. Fertility god or fetish. Stone or clay. Height approximately 3 inches. Note the exaggerated anatomical features which may symbolize "increase."

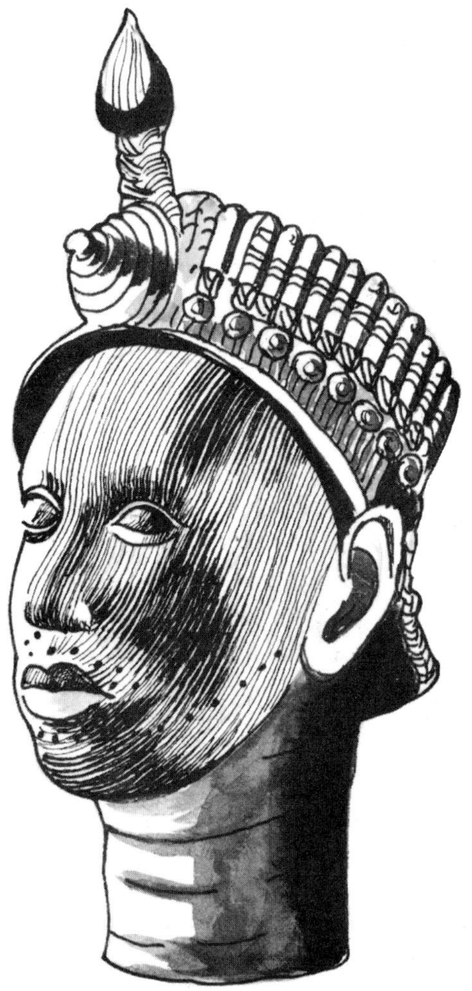

Fig. 9. Ife head. Bronze over clay, created by the "lost wax" process. Height 11 inches. Nigerian classical period of Ife, approximately 12th century. Discovered in an ancient Ife burial ground; now in the British Museum.

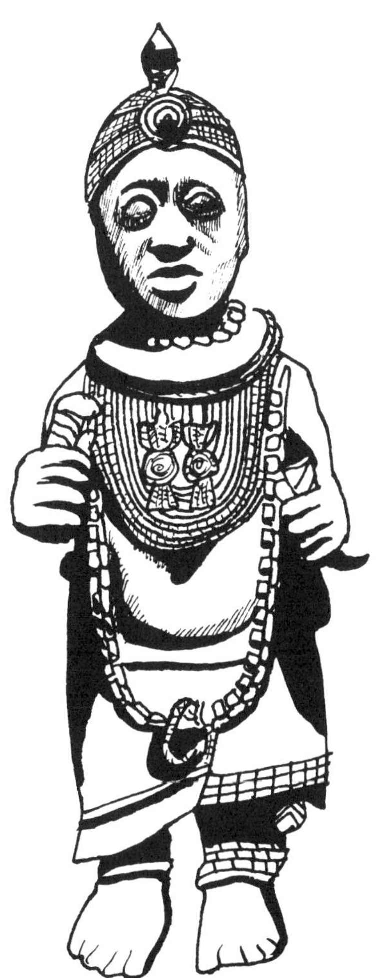

Fig. 10. An Oni (Chieftain) of Ife. Bronze over clay. Height approximately 15 inches. Nigeria, approximately 12th Century. A royal portrait; the ornaments are symbols of wealth and authority; the ax and the horn symbols of power.

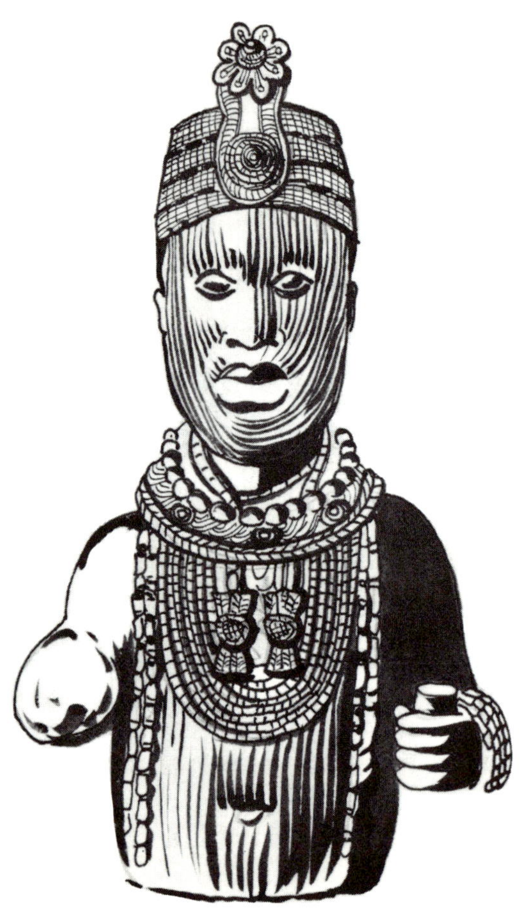

Fig. 11. An Oni of Ife. Bronze over clay. Approximately 15 inches. Another royal portrait. Nigeria. Note the details of ornamentation and the elaborate headdress. Approximately 12th Century.

Traditional Arts

African traditional art represents the expression of pre-literate peoples, usually described as "primitive." From the viewpoint of time, primitive art originated in the dim past of ancient history. From the viewpoint of style or technique, "primitive" may apply to artistic expression of contemporaries after the manner of their forbears or their ancestors. Primitive also connotes "original" or "untutored" or "non-intellectual," but it does not mean unskillful or lacking artistry.

Primitive expression in art is generally conceptual and functional. "Conceptual" means "based on idea" (concept) or special view or essence, an art form which is largely abstract, non-realistic and non-representational. The artist expresses what he thinks the object may be, its peculiar quality or "spirit," rather than what it actually looks like to the casual observer. He does not try to create an imitation which closely resembles the object he depicts. For example, a primitive artist (or an untrained child) in drawing a tree may elongate the central trunk and fashion very short stubby branches as his idea of what the tree actually is. The result may be "tree concept" rather than photographic likeness of a particular tree.

"Functional" means "practically useful" apart from artistic value or attractiveness. First comes practical necessity, mothering invention as it were; the ancient man and woman needed a container to hold water or a pot to cook in so he hollowed out a log to make a crude bucket or he chiseled out a rock or shell to cook his food in. Later he may have shaped it more pleasingly or decorated it with a design or painted it somehow to make it more attractive. "Artistic," after all, first describes something made or something fashioned or created, not necessarily something aesthetically pleasing.

The most ancient artifacts of Africa may have been baskets woven from vines or palms or grasses, or gourds hollowed out to be used as vessels to carry things in. But other ancient artifacts were carvings vaguely representing natural objects and used in magic rites to evoke the strength of the rock or the tree from which they were made, or the fertility of the plant. Carvings of animals or human beings were thought somehow to transfer certain qualities of good or evil, of strength or weakness, from the animal or person represented, or from the object, to the owner or the worshipper. These became "fetish" objects with magical properties.

But to assign any one over-all purpose or objective to the ancient traditional artistic production of Africa would be an invalid over-simplification. Several objectives, rather, are evident from an examination and analysis of ancient African artifacts. One major objective, particularly in rural areas, centers upon religion in the broadest sense of the term; large portions of the "artistic" production were fetish figures or ancestor symbols. The African fetish [Fig. 8], sometimes an oddly shaped stone or a stick in its natural state, was an image of some sort fashioned from materials easily available—wood, stone, or shell—shaped, molded, or carved somehow, distorted into an idealized concept of an animal or a person or another object. Some of the figures resemble human beings with enormous heads or long cylindrical bodies (perhaps hollowed out and containing a "magic powder"), or a protruding belly, perhaps denoting fertility. Each fetish tended to exaggerate a quality considered essential or singularly unique or special. Many fetish figures may have been symbolic representations of ancestors conveying the family spirit or power from past generations to the present. Particularly in the more urban areas where the heads of the tribal "government" resided, another objective was to describe and record, to fashion portraits of rulers living or recently dead to display and to preserve as status symbols or power symbols.

Still another objective may have been aesthetic: to decorate or to make more attractive an abode or a utensil or an ornament for apparel. Even ritual objects like the masks were not always serious, but sometimes were made to entertain and to amuse. Originally the aesthetic may not have been the primary motive for artistic creativity; undoubtedly, however, it supplemented the functional or ritual element, even in the most primitive and ancient forms.

In primitive art the conceptual quality may have been intentional; more than likely the concept may have been non-rational and inspirational, a feeling perhaps rather than an idea. Another theory suggests that the conceptual is the result of a kind of functional abstraction. Because of the constant disintegration of ritual objects owing to the climate and marauding insects as well as man's intentional destruction by burning after ceremonial use, it was frequently necessary to replace the objects. In order to retain the basic characteristics of the original and yet facilitate their reconstruction, only the most essential elements were reproduced, unessential detail was omitted, and abstraction resulted.

Finally, one cannot discount the possibility that some of the conceptual and abstract quality may be due to a lack of skill or understanding of more sophisticated perspective.

However conceived the qualities of conceptual and functional are typical of the primitive artistic expression in Africa.

NIGERIA

In northern Nigeria, buried deep in the earth, small objects in the likeness of human heads and figurines of animals fashioned rather roughly from reddish clay, which had been fired or baked to hardness (a material known as *terra cotta*), have been discovered. [Figs. 3 and 4.] Archaeologists speculate that these were the work of the Nok peoples. The artifacts help to establish the Nok as the most ancient of datable African cultures, perhaps existing well over two thousand years ago. Many other clay figures may still be buried and undiscovered. These few *terra cotta* samplings are of rough texture, revealing rudimentary features with flat noses, open staring eyes, lipless mouths. The head-dresses, however, are rather more elaborate. Despite the rudimentary shapes, the figures are expressive and distinctive.

More famous are the figures in *terra cotta* and the bronzed sculptured portraits of Yoruba chieftains and warriors discovered in the Southwest Region of Nigeria at Ife [Figs. 6, 10, 11], a place held sacred by the Yoruba as being the exact spot where the earth was shaped and man created. The Ife artifacts coincide roughly with the Middle Ages in western cultural epochs, dating probably from the eleventh to the fifteenth centuries.

The *terra cotta* figures of Ife are much more realistic than those of the earlier Nok culture; the eyes are carefully fashioned, the noses and the mouths well shaped, the tribal skin markings clearly defined. One of the Ife figures is the head of a beautiful woman, in some ways recalling the famous head of the Egyptian Nefertite, although the Ife head is badly damaged and fragmentary. Later replicas of the same head have been discovered.

The bronzed figures are obviously not as old as the terra cotta heads discovered in the north. The materials and the technique appear to be more complex and sophisticated. We cannot know their original creators, but we can speculate about the method of fashioning them by analyzing the result.

Cire perdue or "lost wax" is the name of the process or the technique the Yoruba employed in fashioning these bronzes. It was an intricate process—one that may be somehow symbolic of the manner in which basic original African art eventually became coated over with successive layers of another culture.

In the lost wax process, a clay model was shaped and molded and then evenly covered with a thin layer of wax. This in turn was covered over again with a layer of clay and ashes and then backed by more clay. Hollow pipes were inserted through the layers of clay into the layer of wax at top and bottom. The whole business was placed in a sort of crude oven or propped up on sticks and baked over hot coals. The layers of clay hardened over the heat and the wax melted and drained out through the hollow pipes (hence the name "lost wax"). Next, hot liquid bronze, a mixture of copper and tin, was poured through the hollow pipes into the opening left by the melted wax. Thus a kind of thin bronze shell formed over the original clay model. When this had dried and the outer clay was chipped off, the more durable bronze covering could be smoothed off and the features sharpened up and a sculptured head fashioned which would resist destruction. Possibly the peculiarly serrated stripping on some of the faces was molded in the original clay model or perhaps it was gouged out later by a sharp instrument.

The *cire perdue* process may have been uniquely African; more probably it was also discovered independently in other parts of the world. In any event, it reveals the skill of early African craftsmen and helps dispel the misconception that these primitive artists were inexpert and crude.

The bronzes made by this process and discovered at Ife have exquisitely fine features and are less abstract and conceptual than earlier artifacts. The eyes, however, are somewhat abstracted, like the finest work of Michelangelo, and they have a slightly slanted or oriental cast (one notices this characteristic frequently in African sculpture). Some have serrated skin markings forming decorative design over the entire surface of the face; others lack these tribal markings entirely. Peculiarly characteristic is the series of small holes about the mouth and extending up the sides of the chin in some of the figures. Perhaps these once held stones or beads for decoration or perhaps even bits of human hair for beards. [Fig. 9.] One frequently photographed portrait includes fragments of two arms, one grasping a horn or cup. [Fig.

10.] Details of an elaborate headdress, necklaces and beads, a twin-figured medallion insignia, and facial and body serrations are clearly discernable. Another Ife figure wears a beaded crown ornamented with a protruding bud-like object. The facial expression is serene and dignified befitting a royal personage. [Fig. 9.]

So artistic and seemingly sophisticated are these Ife bronzes that early critics and archaeologists advanced the theory they must have been created by some visiting European Renaissance artist.(1) The terms "classic" and "elegant" are used to describe them.

Equally skillful and famous are the bronzes by Benin craftsmen [Figs. 12-16] said to have been instructed by artisans brought from Ife as teachers. But the Benin bronzes seem clearly to belong to a later period, corresponding roughly to the Renaissance of European culture, and therefore belong more properly to the period of Colonial Arts.

The Yoruba were myth makers. Like other primitives they believed a spirit resides within or behind all things. And they believed the spirit or power could behave in surprising and unpredictable ways.(2) They discovered or fashioned objects which evoked the spirit or encased it or contained it. Yorubas practiced ancestor worship, with a carved staff, or "ofo," passed along from generation to generation to symbolize the power held sacred for a whole tribe or several tribes. Each river, each tree, each valley was thought to have a spirit, and each spirit had its priest who presumably knew the secret rites necessary to evoke that power, who carved out images and made masks appropriate to the season or the place or the thing itself. The priest also devised appropriate dances and chants.

The sacred symbols which today may be considered art objects were used in connection with the dancing and the chanting. More often than not these ceremonies were preliminary to a sacrifice of some sort —among some of the Yoruba cults the sacrifice of a dog, perhaps to "Ogun," the god of war. The sacrifice was a kind of release or purging or considered a "scapegoat" ritual that through sublimation relieved certain individuals or the group as a whole from dangerous social pressures.(3)

Although there were different priests for each spirit the special "Diviner" or "Dibia" could be the same for several villages. The Dibia gave advice concerning which spirit to sacrifice to and with what special rites and symbols. Because each individual had the right to choose his own Dibia, sacred symbols from one village might become interchanged with those of another village.(4)

The Benin Obas with their magnificent ceremonial dress and ornaments and symbols demonstrate the use of objects as a display of power. In ancient times the power was accompanied by bloody sacrifice horrible to relate—yet in some strange way these sacrifices gave a kind of comfort for the subjects: the absolute ruthlessness of the sacrifice demonstrated a power which could provide protection for those under the ruler's jurisdiction.(5) There is a legend, for instance, of a general of an ancient Yoruba tribe who sacrificed his own son and had his skin stretched on a drum—possibly to show his power and authority. Any ruler who placed his office above his family could perhaps be trusted never to place personal interests above those of society. One is reminded of the sacrifice of Iphigenia by Agamemnon in Greek legend, of Creon's argument in Sophocles' *Antigone,* and of the projected sacrifice of Isaac by his father Abraham in the Old Testament.

Few examples of wood sculpture survive because time disintegrates wood or it gets eaten up by ants. Archaeologists surmise, however, there were many wooden "fetish" figures—some of them very crude, some of them studded with nails or rubbed with the stains of "medicine."

The strength or energy or power evoked by the use of the object in a ritual or a ceremony was considered more important than the object itself or the person who fashioned the object. A peculiar custom, to western views, occurred commonly in Africa: after their use the mask or the fetish employed was burned or otherwise destroyed by the priests themselves, then re-made or re-fashioned for the next occasion, since it was believed that the spirit or power had "gone out of" the original. Even today ancestral objects of veneration are sometimes destroyed every other generation or so by the families who venerate them. It may be that this custom is a kind of symbolic concept of renewal or resurrection—to destroy the old and replace it with the new.

The custom of destruction and renewal in Africa may account for the disappearance of many African artifacts, the constant need to train skilled craftsmen to replace destroyed objects, and perhaps also for the apparent disinterest in preserving objects considered as receptacles for a strength or a power only temporarily, a power which in itself was indestructible.

The Fetish

Perhaps no one understands precisely how the concept of the fetish originated or indeed understands completely the extent of its symbolic meaning. Apparently fetish figures are considered both symbol and receptacle for a spirit or power which in some mysterious way affects the creator of the figure or its owner with special "increase" of power—in strength or fertility. Even the initiates of the secret cults in which they were used may have understood only vaguely how the fetish worked, and surely the uninitiated foreigner could not penetrate the zealously guarded "magic" secrets. Foreigners sometimes found fetish objects they considered artistic or ethnologically curious. They removed them to their museums for display as aesthetic objects or for ethnic studies. This pilfering of sacred objects out of Africa was in one sense a scandal, the desecration of the religion of another race. In another sense it was a blessing, for otherwise these evidences of an ancient culture would not have survived.

The tradition of creating or of discovering fetish objects (for they were sometimes found rather than fashioned) persists in contemporary African tribal groups. Quite possibly the entire concept of African sculpture may be bound up with the concept of the fetish. This may be further evidence that traditional African art was primarily both conceptual and functional, rather than aesthetic or decorative. The fetish object itself was not for contemplation alone, nor was it considered aesthetic or decorative apart from its function.

The idea of "fertility"—in the larger area of its meaning, that is, as "an increase" of some sort—is basic to the concept of the fetish. Figures fashioned to be worn as the top of an elaborate headdress which covered the head with a mask of wood or of cloth, perhaps decorated with beads or cowrie shells, somehow not only disguised but transformed the wearer, especially when he performed the movements of a sacred dance or ceremonial rite or chanted incantations to the rhythmic beating of drums. Some indescribable upsurging of energy was experienced—call it power, strength, potency, growth, increase, or "fertility." The mask or statuette fashioned for this purpose (or the bit of shell or oddly shaped stone that had been discovered) served only as the casement or container within which the magical property somehow mysteriously resided. The fetish was inextricably interrelated with the process of creation or with the movements of the dance or the chanting of the ritual. The process or functional use completed the "magic."

One might find an analogy without stretching the facts too far in the Christian concept of the Reliquary—a case containing the sacred bone of a martyred saint, which for some believers transmits the spiritual power of the saint if touched with reverence and with faith. Or indeed an analogy can also be drawn from the concept of the Eucharist in the ceremony of the Mass, when the bit of bread and wine symbolize the body and the blood of Christ, transmitting spiritual significance to the faithful.

The African craftsman became the medium for conveying the power of the God—a kind of priest using special tools held sacred for that purpose, working in secret in a special building apart from the rest of the tribe, living, during the period of his creation at least, as a sort of recluse, waited upon by certain women of the tribe who were bound by taboo never to look upon him.

And apparently the primitive artist-craftsman-priest, as he concentrated upon carving the mask or fashioning the fetish image, worked at times in a sort of divine trance or frenzy, evoking the god-force or sacred energy and translating, transforming or transferring it to the object he fashioned. The mystique of all this is not clearly understood, but there recurs the idea that the artist (or indeed the performer of a sacred dance or ritual or the drummer on the tom-tom) is inspired by some outside force which descends upon him so that he creates partly by means of this inspiration. This is, of course, not unlike the concept of the ancient Greeks who believed that the Muse of Apollo inspired their artists. And indeed some modern artists refer to the fact that their work "turned out rather well" as if it had been at least partially shaped by another force!

The identity of the traditional African artist is rarely known, perhaps because once he had evoked the power, he as individual artist became unimportant. Whereas in countries primarily Christian, the emphasis is upon the significance of the individual, in Africa traditionally the emphasis has been upon the family, the ancestors, the clan, the tribe. Westerners tend to think in terms of absolutes; the dichotomy of right or wrong, truth or error, material or spiritual—to label precisely and to include or exclude positively. The non-Christian African—like the non-Christian Oriental—tends to think in terms far less absolute or determinate, with reference to the ambivalence of all things, the many-sided aspects of the truth. Buddha has a thousand faces in the Orient; a fetish object in Africa emphasizes and exaggerates a special feature relative to a ceremonial or a concept. Each object may harbor, temporarily perhaps, a portion of the total power or strength for good or evil, but the energy may depart and go elsewhere and find abode in another fetish or mask.

Today among certain peoples in Africa and elsewhere in the world, largely among primitive peoples, fetishes are regarded with superstitious reverence and held in high esteem, shrouded with mystery and surrounded by rigid "taboos" or restrictions concerning their use and function. For instance, according to one taboo, one must never look directly upon some fetish objects, and, therefore, these fetish objects are kept hidden under coverings of cloth; according to another taboo, one must never touch certain portions of the fetish or never approach it with unclean hands or after shedding blood. Many fetish taboos forbid women to have anything to do with fetish rites and women were known to have been put to death for even inadvertently and unintentionally observing the fetish by accident!

MUSIC

Because we have no record of the musical sounds produced out of the ancient past in Africa or elsewhere, we can only surmise what the ancient music was like by supposing that modern tribal musicians reflect ancient tradition. We can never really know what African music was like in ancient times any more than we can be certain what the music of ancient Greece sounded like. (Perhaps some day scientists will devise a method of picking up the vibrations of sound waves out of the past and thus satisfy our curiosity. The possibility seems no more fantastic or remote than putting a man on the moon!)

In a book entitled *Among the Ibos* written in 1920, George T. Basden, a missionary who lived in Nigeria for many years, writes this account of traditional African music:

How long they [the Ibo people] have been performers upon the instruments now in use, and who invented them, are questions to which answers are not forthcoming. As the people of the interior have never, until very recent times, had any intercourse with the civilised world, we conclude that their musical proclivities, their instruments and their songs, remain practically as they existed in primitive times, or at any rate that they have developed spontaneously. . . .

The simplest and most primitive instrument is the "ugene"—a kind of whistle. It is made of baked clay, in shape round, and about the size of a billiard ball. A substitute is occasionally used, cut from a piece of ukpadi wood. It has two holes, one at the top which serves as the mouthpiece: the other at the front for measuring and varying the piped notes. . . .

The custom of transmitting signals by sounds is a common one, and is not confined to these whistles. The chiefs entitled to carry ivory horns send out messages by powerful blasts of dot-and-dash (Morse) notes. The horns are blown flute-wise, and the note can be varied in length, but not in tone. The chiefs are adept in the art of trumpeting on the horns and use them for communicating quite long messages. More often they perform upon them purely for display, especially in assemblies, and the din created by half a dozen chiefs in full blast is deafening. A big supply of breath is required, but a satisfactory result depends entirely on the proper use of the lips.

Other methods of spreading information are practiced, notably by the beating of tom-toms, of which more will be said later, and by simply whistling with the lips. Men can communicate with one another quite freely by this method when completely out of speaking range. Boys early find out how to prepare whistles from grass stems, and some of the youths can imitate bugle calls in a very clever manner by blowing down the hollow stalks of a freshly cut pawpaw leaf.

Besides these I know of but one other wind instrument—the "awja," a reed some six inches in length furnished with three holes for fingering—one in front, one at the back for the thumb, and the bottom outlet. It is always used in assemblies of men, especially when a big piece of work is in progress. The instrumentalist sits down on one side and blows vigorously through the pipe; the tones are shrill and piercing, and at times peculiarly trying to the nerves.

. . . The tom-toms are mostly nothing but hollow blocks of wood; the sound carries a long distance in a country where there is no vehicular traffic and no roar of industry to deaden it. The big tom-toms (ekwe) are not intended to be instruments of music, but are used chiefly for spreading information for certain ceremonial purposes, and at sacrificial festivals; meetings are called by their use, and various announcements proclaimed. An ekwe is in great request when a man proceeds to the highest titular degree. On completion of all the business connected with the taking of the Awzaw title, the fact is communicated by beating the tom-tom. The smaller tom-toms may be of similar pattern, or they may be wooden cylinders with skin stretched over one end, the most prized—and now rather rare—being those covered with human skin. In the old days it was not uncommon for human victims to be flayed alive and their skins converted into drum-heads.

Some of the drums are of smaller pattern. They are distinguished from the ekwe and are technically known as ufie. Steady application for a long period is necessary in order to become a qualified performer on these. The performer must know his instrument thoroughly, and be able to gauge the differences in sound to be extracted from the whole top surface of the drum. Each square inch around the slotted opening in the cylinder has its own peculiar note, and these notes are further supplemented by fingering. Often two drums are used simultaneously and the hands cross and recross like those of a cavalry drummer; hence, although to the European tom-toms are apt to become monotonous and wearisome, yet it must be allowed that the native exponent exhibits great skill in beating his tattoo upon it. To him, indeed, the beating of the instrument is always significant; something is conveyed to the native mind which is utterly incomprehensible to the European, and our inability to grasp that meaning in no way detracts from the importance of the drum in every Ibo function. . . .

The "ubaw" is an instrument which cannot be compared with any foreign one with which I am acquainted. It is composed of thin pieces of a very soft wood (okwe) and in shape resembles an oblong box. It is from five to fifteen inches long, from four to six inches wide, and from one to two inches deep; thus far it is similar in principle to a violin, but in lieu of strings thin strips of offolaw [a fibrous bamboo] are used. These are fixed at the tail-end and then pass over a low bridge to which they are also bound. The loose ends are cut to different lengths and separated widely enough to permit freedom in fingering. The instrument is held in both hands, with the tail piece pointing away from the person, and the thumbs are used for manipulating the strips of bamboo. The thumbs press cleanly on the strips and are then slipped sharply backwards, and a twanging sound results, the notes varying according to the different lengths of the six or eight keys of the instrument. Occasionally loosely threaded cowrie shells are attached to the tail end of the ubaw, which are shaken to make an accompaniment. . . .

Probably the most interesting of the Ibo instruments is the "ubaw-akwala," a sort of primitive guitar. . . . It has a triangular-shaped body formed by sewing together three pieces of soft wood with fibre. To the under part from four to eight pliable canes of different lengths are securely laced, all of them extending well beyond the head of the instrument. They are then bent upwards and the strings are tied to the ends, crossed over the bridge, and finally fastened to the tail-piece. The strings (awmi) are pieces of fibre taken from the base of the palm tree and carefully rubbed down to the required fineness. The instrument is held like the ubaw, but the method of playing is different, the thumbs lightly twanging the strings, the left and right working an equal number of them. It has rather a sweet sound, not unlike light staccato notes from a violin. The instrument is tuned by bending the canes and passing the strings one or more times round them until the desired pitch is secured. The musician must learn all tunes by ear, or compose his own, which he frequently does.

The ubaw-akwala is the favourite instrument for accompanying songs and chants, and is particularly favoured by strolling singers at night. One is often awakened by the pleasant strains of a party of musicians on their rounds.

Instrumental soloists of any reputation, especially performers on the awja and ekwe, are treated with great respect, their services are in demand and their reward is generally liberal. Talent is recognised and many artists become very popular. From a musical point of view one is inclined to think that the native singing is more fascinating than the instrumental music. It is doubtful whether there are any proper songs, but there are a great number of established refrains and recitatives. The leader of a chorus is accorded much the same honour amongst the Ibos as that granted to the minstrel in ancient days in England. He must possess not only the musical gift but the poetical instinct also. He creates his theme as the song proceeds, and great ingenuity is displayed in fitting words to time and tune on the spur of the moment. Any unusual incident is seized upon and utilized as material by the leader, and when this fails he has recourse to retelling, in song, the exploits of old.(6)

Kenya

In northern Kenya in some totally abandoned scrub land around the shores of Lake Rudolph various "petrographs" or wall engravings on caves or cliffs depict the human figure or animals, notably the giraffe —that fantastically graceful long-necked creature which abounds today in Kenya and continues to intrigue native and tourist alike. The drawings, many of them crude and indistinct, date back to the stone age.

In the interior of Kenya very few examples of art fashioned by ancient tribes have been discovered—perhaps because they have not been searched for hard enough; perhaps, and more likely, because the artifacts made of wood or woven from grasses disintegrated. Clay figures in roughly human form called "nungu," probably very old, exist in the area around Wachaya in the district of Kilimanjaro. Some of these figures supported pots or vessels on their heads apparently for ceremonial rites or sacrifices. Funeral posts to mark or commemorate the graves of the ancestors, elaborately painted and carved with geometric designs and partially abstracted human heads piled atop each other like the totem poles of the American Indians are created by contemporary Bantu tribes in Kenya. These undoubtedly reflect the traditional ancient practice, but the originals are gone. Similarly the masks of contemporary Kenyan tribal secret societies probably reflect the art of the past.

Shield designs of the contemporary Kikuyu tribes also reflect the practices from the traditional past: the patterns appear to be left to the fancy of the painter rather than to be symbols of a clan or tribe. [Fig. 34.] A characteristic line-interlinking-motif is regularly present on the inside surface, however, and this, according to legend, was taught by the god to the primordial ancestor of all Kikuyu. The motif occurs also on the naked bodies of dancers.(7) Black, red, brown and white are the typical colors employed.

Theatre, in the western conventional sense, probably did not occur in ancient Africa. But singing and dancing and pantomimic story-telling surely existed, performed at times by specially selected and trained performers and for certain festivals or rituals by untrained members of the cult or by the initiates.

This account by Jomo Kenyatta in *Facing Mount Kenya* describes the "Great Ceremonial Dance (Matuumo)" performed by boys and girls at the coming-of-age circumcision ritual; it quite probably reflects traditional custom.

The girl is provided with a bell (*kegamba*) which is tied on her right leg just above the calf, or sometimes above the knee, to provide the rhythm to the procession and also for the dance. The girl is put in the middle of the procession, which moves slowly, singing ritual songs until they reach the *irua's* [the initiate about to be circumcised] homestead, where the procession is joined by the other initiates who are accompanied by other processions of relatives and friends dressed in their best.

The *matuumo* dances and songs begin at forenoon before the sun is overhead and continue the whole day. It takes place inside the homestead, but if the homestead is not large enough it is held on some convenient site which must be in close proximity to the homestead. The site is cleared and carefully examined to make sure that there is nothing on the ground that can hurt the feet of candidates while dancing.

The ceremonial doctor (*mondo-mogo wa mambura*) goes round the site sprinkling a brownish powder called *rothuko* on the ground, to counteract any evil design which might be directed against the candidates. This is followed by the elders who sprinkle honey beer (*njoohi ya ooke*) on the ground to appease the ancestral spirits and to bring them into harmony with those of the living. When the elders have completed their work of purifying the ground, the initiates enter the ground accompanied by their sponsors, relatives and friends, adorned with ceremonial dresses and green leaves; then all of them begin to dance. The crowd which has gathered for the great event forms a thick wall round the arena. While the dancing and singing is going on a ceremonial horn is blown at intervals, and before it is sounded, a little medicine (*itwanda*) is rubbed inside; this medicine is believed to have power of chasing away evil spirits and preventing them from doing harm to the initiates.

Late in the afternoon an arch of banana trees and sugarcanes is built at the entrance of the homestead of the *matuumo*. The arch is decorated with sacred flowers of many shapes and colour; no unauthorised person may pass through the arch. The arch is considered as a medium through which the ancestral spirits can be harmonised with the *irua* and appeased, so as not to bring any misfortune on the ceremony in which the ceremonial council offers sacrifices to the god Ngai.

When the decoration of the arch is finished the dance is stopped. The *irua* candidates are lined up ready for the sacrifice which marks the end of *matuumo*. This consists of the boys running a race of about two miles to a sacred tree called *mogumo* or *motamayo*, which they have to climb and break top branches, while the girls gather round singing, and at the same time gathering the leaves and the twigs dropped by the boys.

To start the race a ceremonial horn is blown. At this point the girls, who are not allowed to participate in the race, start out walking to the tree, escorted by a group of senior warriors and women singing ritual and heroic songs. When the girls are near the tree, the ceremonial horn is again sounded, this time indicating that it is time for the boys to start the race. The boys then start running in a great excitement, as though they were going to a battle. The truth is, it is really considered a sort of fight between the spirit of childhood and that of adulthood.

The crowd which has already gathered round the tree await the arrival of the boys in order to judge the winner of the race. They shout and cheer merrily as the excited boys arrive, raising their wooden spears, ready to throw them over the sacred tree. The significance of this ceremonial racing is the fact that it determines the leader of that particular age-group. The one who reaches the tree first and throws his wooden spear over the tree is elected there and then as the leader and the spokesman of the age-group for life. It is believed that such a one is chosen by the will of the ancestral spirits in communication with Ngai, and is therefore highly respected.

The girl who arrives at the sacred tree first is also regarded in the same way. She becomes the favourite, and all try to win her affections with the hope of marrying her.

The *mogumo* ceremony occupies only a short time. As stated above, the boys climb the tree, break the top branches, while the girls collect leaves and twigs dropped on the ground. These are later tied into bunches and carried back to the homestead to keep the sacred fire burning the whole night and also to be used in other rituals, especially in making the initiates' beds. The songs rendered by the relatives and friends round the foot of the tree generally pertain to sexual knowledge. This is to give the initiates an opportunity of acquainting themselves with all necessary rules and regulations governing social relationship between men and women.

At the completion of *kuuna mogumo* (breaking of the sacred tree), the boys and girls are lined up according to the order of their adoption. Here a ceremony of taking the tribal oath (*muma wa anake*) is conducted by the elders of the ceremonial council. The initiates promise by this oath that from this day onward they will in every respect deport themselves like adults and take all responsibilities in the welfare of the community, and that they will not lag behind whenever called upon to perform any service or duty in the protection and advancement of the tribe as a whole. Furthermore, they are made to promise never to reveal the tribal secrets, even to a member of the tribe who has not yet been initiated.

At the conclusion of the oath ceremony a group of senior warriors form at the head of the procession, followed by the initiates. Then the crowd flanks both sides of the procession as a bodyguard. They march slowly towards the homestead of the *matuumo,* carrying the leaves and twigs gathered from the sacred tree, *mogumo.* The initiates are warned never to look behind as they move along, for to do so would bring misfortune to them at the time of *irua,* and, furthermore, the childhood misdeeds which they have thrown over the sacred tree, *mogumo,* would come back to them. The songs they sing on the homeward march are directed towards denouncing all things that are not fit and proper for any adult member of the community to do. Moreoever, the phrases embodied in these songs are to encourage the initiates to become worthy and honourable members of the adult community into which they are to be graduated.(8)

The songs and dances and the symbolic pantomime surrounding this coming-of-age ritual contain the essence of theatre. Upon many other occasions the ceremonial with song and dancing accompanied by the rhythmic beating of the drum had the characteristic of transformation or make-believe which is theatrical—preparing the participants for an experience, celebrating a harvest, propitiating a god. And portions of the ceremony must have proved entertaining as well as instructive or emotionally inspiring. The ceremonial was functional as part of a ritual or a celebration; it was artistic in the sense that it was planned and prepared for; the patterns of the songs and the dances, although not rigidly set, were passed along year by year from generation to generation.

Republic of Zaire

Ancient primitive art in the vast area of the Republic of Zaire, where a recent census indicates over fifteen million people live divided into four major ethnic groups, cannot be easily characterized or even listed efficiently. The astonishing variations of style in artistic expression become more clearly understandable when one considers the fact that although the Bantu peoples are the largest ethnic group in modern Zaire there are nearly two hundred distinguishable separate dialects among this single ethnic group. An official publication of the Zaire Consulate lists four major traditional artistic regions and attempts to divide these into ten distinctive groupings.(9) There may have been many more or fewer than these in ancient times.

These vast regions produced some wood carvings but the white ant and the climate destroyed the evidences; only those objects removed to the safety of museums or those created by contemporaries presumably after the manner of the traditional can be studied and analyzed. One has to make assumptions from these concerning the nature of the lost originals.

Concerning the characteristics of traditional Zarien wood-carvings, these statements may be valid; essentially conceptual, the individual facial features identifiable as specific persons are lacking. A kind of rigidity of posture and a static expression occurs, not only in the nail fetishes [Fig. 17] but also in the little maternity statues of mother and child. The mother holding and perhaps nursing the child has a kind of remote, immutable expression, gazing straight ahead and apparently not even aware of the child. Tribal markings are evident; hair styles, facial scarifications are carefully depicted, distinguishing tribe from tribe rather than individual from individual. Enlargement of the head out of proportion to the remainder of the body and truncated legs and feet seem typical. The masks also appear rigid and with fixed expression, somehow less expressive than masks from other regions of Africa. [Figs. 20-23.]

Among the objects preserved in museums and identified as having been produced in ancient times are examples of the nail fetishes [Fig. 17]; drums of various shapes and sizes—some of them covered with human skin; fly switches with decorative handles; headrests and benches—some of them elaborately carved in the shape of male/female figures facing each other and supporting the headrest or seat on their heads [Fig. 25]; combs; engraved calabashes (gourds); ivory masks; ritual libation pots. And distinctive among Zarien people of the northwest are coffins in the shape of huge insects.

Fourteen museums of ethnic culture in the Zarien Republic preserve and display such objects and the Art Museum at Muchenge is reserved almost exclusively for traditional objects considered aesthetically important by twentieth century experts. Currently nine Folkloric Groups under government sponsorship investigate, collect, and preserve ancient artifacts.

Since modern Zaire is frequently called "a musical paradise" it may well be that ancient artistic expression was characteristically musical —the most ephemeral of all the arts and the least preservable. Efforts are being made today to record on tape and film many of the traditional chants, the ceremonial drumming and the dances and pantomimic rites as currently practiced after the manner of ancient forebears.

The traditional music of Zaire, like that of all black Africa and indeed most every ancient culture, was primarily vocal, largely monophonic and folk—folk in the sense that it was not written down and resulted from a group composition and not a single composer. Rhythm rather than melody predominates and percussion instruments played an important role to provide the rhythms. Four kinds of percussion instruments in use today undoubtedly are of ancient origin [Fig. 28, 29, 30]:

Idiophones: long tubes of wood or metal open at one end which are struck against the ground to produce a hollow sound—the length and size of the tube varies the pitch somewhat; wooden drums with longitudinal openings; various bells of iron or wood; a kind of xylophone made from wooden slats which are struck with mallets.

Membranophones: Drums made from skins stretched over a hollow log and attached with nails.

Chordophones: simple musical bows with or without sounding gourds. These are plucked to cause the taut cord to vibrate; a kind of bowed harp or lyre with several taut strings (used in the northern area).

Aerophones: the antlers of different types of antelopes fashioned into flutes, and several kinds of whistles made from wood or reed.

Supplementing finger snapping and hand-clapping, variations of these primitive instruments provided rhythmic accompaniment to chants and songs which reflected everyday happenings, which evoked a mood or produced an attitude to support a religious ritual, or which became an incantation to promote fertility. Dancing and dramatic representation in pantomimic form evidently occurred simultaneously, either by design or spontaneously.

The percussive instruments communicated rhythmically and emphatically and also quite literally conveyed meaning—a kind of symbolic language felt rather than intellectually understood. The "talking drums" of Africa by tradition were the voices of the gods speaking through the performers.

Large buildings and gigantic monuments like the pyramids of Egypt at Gizeh and the Collossi in the Valley of the Kings may not be the only or indeed the best examples of a civilization. The talking drums of Africa and the wonderfully subtle percussive music which modern musicologists only dimly understand but vastly appreciate may likewise be strong evidence of an artistic culture—and the poetic expression of a people who never wrote it down.

Oral "Literature"

Africa has not until very recently been given much status as a "literate" continent. This may, of course, be another illustration of the "provincialism" of western cultures and of the fallacy of a too narrow definition of terms. Obviously even in the West the origins of what eventually became a literary heritage were not at first written down. Most literatures stem from pre-literate oral traditions. The legendary Homer of Ancient Greece, for instance, may never actually have existed, and if he did he must have been largely an editor or compiler of the legends comprising *The Iliad* and *The Odyssey,* which were originally spoken or chanted by minstrels to the accompaniment of the lyre at festivals and banquets. These were folk tales told around the fireside, handed down from father to son, or from professional story-teller to professional story-teller.

In Africa, where there has always been a multiplicity of languages, but very few that could be written down until recent times, an "oral literature" developed which was both prolific and influential. Contemporary researchers have already uncovered over 7,000 stories and tales from Africa, varying in length and significance.(10) The chronology of these tales is almost impossible to check because the oral tradition in Africa covers so many centuries, so many areas and so many different versions in so many languages.

Regional or epochal characteristics or trends, therefore, or labels or patterns, are probably impossible to classify or describe with any degree of accuracy. As with other forms of traditional art in Africa such analysis must be based upon speculation or supposition about the relatively few samplings which have been discovered and preserved, translated or recorded. A vast amount of material is as yet undiscovered or has been irretrievably lost. Concerning the literature of Ancient Greece we have the evidence of Aristotle to testify to the work of many tragic dramatists, but the plays of only three Greek tragedians are extant. Similarly we have so far only a sampling of African stories.

Based on this admittedly insufficient evidence, there seem to be more similarities with characteristics of Western literary tradition than differences; there are few characteristics uniquely African. The general subject matter results from experience and from the environment and from the imagination; it is a description of conditions, a protest against them, an advocacy, or a combination of these. The techniques and methods of narration become more elaborate and heightened into poetry when emotions are touched deeply; they cross over into theatre and dance when gesture and pantomime supplement voice to emphasize emotion and increase empathy.

The specific subjects range from animal stories to stories of the supernatural which are clearly related to the environment and the everyday experience of Africans who live close to animals, the forest, and the soil and who observe with curiosity and concern the apparently malevolent or benign aspects of nature, which sometimes opposes and sometimes supports the endeavors of man. African tales include explanations of the way things are and the way they came to be so, as well as speculations about how they ought to be, and complaints against injustice and warnings to the unwary. They also concern the dilemma in making a decision when the avenues of choice are difficult or dangerous. There are tales of superhuman strength and deeds of daring. Favorite topics include the trickery of the wily weakling or the infant prodigy who outwits the more slow-thinking but stronger opponent or deflates the arrogance of the more sophisticated: the spider, for instance, against the hyena, the hare (or rabbit) against the elephant, puny little man against the monster-ogre.

Among the Bantus the hare is hero; among the people of Zaire the gazelle; among the Hausa the spider, with the hyena as the greedy, stupid butt of the tales. Surely the Uncle Remus stories popular in America and a whole tradition of animal stories can be traced to African origins as well as to Aesop. Many such stories were brought to

Europe and the West by African slaves who adapted them to suit the new environment and occasion.

Concerning the objectives of these traditional African tales, one might speculate that they were intended not only for a social or a moral or a religious purpose but also for entertainment. That there were "professional" story-tellers is supported by the practices of present-day African tribal custom. That there were also many tellers of tales who were not professional is characteristically human: a father tells his son his experiences with certain embellishments and soon fact borders upon fiction. A mother relates to a son or a daughter both her experiences and her emotion. Story-tellers undoubtedly acquire reputations for pantomime and elaborate use of appropriate and varying tones of voice to heighten their stories and to enhance the illusion of reality. Frequently, humor was interjected; there is an almost child-like lack of sentimentality. Like most folk stories these are remarkably concise; at times transitions are omitted and conclusions are abrupt and indecisive.

Although there is no single truly authentic version of any particular story from the oral tradition in Africa, because each teller of a tale added his own variations, the thread of similarity which runs through the various versions is surprising.

Swahili and Hausa languages are perhaps the best known and most widely spoken native African languages. Hausa-speaking peoples are mostly concentrated in northern Nigeria but they spread across the continent in both directions and there is a sizeable group of Hausa speaking people in Zaire.

A selection of Hausa stories of various types is included here. These may be as "characteristic" as any group of traditional African tales can be. A number of other works might have been selected; these were chosen because they seem to illustrate both the universal and the unique in subject matter and in technique. One must take into account, however, the fact that in translating, contemporary writers may have altered not only the language but quite possibly attitudes or tempers or styles of the originals. These stories are only a surface sampling but perhaps they indicate the degree of artistic merit the original versions may have had.

SUMMARY

At the risk of "trying to capture the wind in a sieve" and recognizing the possibility that it may be a gross oversimplification, the work of traditional African artists in Kenya, Zaire, and Nigeria might be summarized according to its objectives or function something like this:

(1) Objects created for magical or ritualistic rites in which the creation and the function became inextricably interwoven, the act of creating and the effect of the thing created occurring simultaneously.

(2) Objects devised for status or to reveal power, like the portrait statues of Yoruba chieftains and the amulets and tokens of office.

(3) Objects concerned with potency or increase—"fertility" in the larger sense—as with fetish images, the masks and sculptures involving the increase in productivity of the soil or of the hunt or of sex.

(4) Objects involving a record or a commemoration like the funeral posts and the Ife royal bronzes.

(5) Objects and ceremonials involving entertainment, for currently the renditions of traditional dances and chants, using masks and costumes and other decorative or ornamental or ritual symbols are amusing and enjoyed both by performer and observer. In Africa the concept of religion has never been entirely somber and dour but rather filled with shouts of laughter and exuberance.

(6) Objects for functional use (pots for cooking, baskets, etc.) made aesthetically pleasing by decoration.

Traditional African Folklore (The Oral Tradition)

These selections are samples from the enormous oral literary tradition of Africa. Regionally they are from areas which are today the countries of Nigeria, the Democratic Republic of Zaire, and Kenya. They are folk in the sense they have no known original authorship and were only recently written down. There are no "authentic" versions; many of these tales treat the same subject, varying the details and the ornamentation. They are concise, objective and singularly free of sentimentality; even in the translation they reveal something of the artistic skill in narration as well as the viewpoints and subject matter which may be at the same time uniquely African and also universal in appeal.

The Spider and the Hyena

Gizo the spider and Koki his wife were once living in a town where people grew nothing but ground-nuts.

When the rains came all the farmers went out to plant seed. 'Husband' said Koki to Gizo 'the rains have broken—you know you ought to start planting our ground-nuts.'

'Koki' said the spider 'that is just what I intend to do.'

With that he gave her three thousand cowries to buy seed ground-nuts and when she returned with them he told her to roast them.

'What?' said his wife. 'Who ever heard of roasting seed?'

'Koki' said the spider 'you meddle too much—just do as I tell you.' So Koki roasted the nuts and then the spider told her to put them in a mortar and pound them into a paste, adding pepper and salt.

When she had finished the spider set off for his farm with a hoe and a water-bottle and the ground-nut paste. There he found a large tree and, stretching himself out in the shade, spent the whole day eating and drinking. Towards evening he got up, dirtied his clothes, and returned to his house.

'Welcome home' said Koki, but the spider only swore at her. 'What do you mean "Welcome"?' he said 'Just you get me some hot water so that I can wash.'

Time passed and the season for hoeing came round. 'People have started hoeing, Gizo' said Koki. 'When are you going to begin?'

'My dear Koki' said the spider 'ground-nuts should be left among the weeds—that way they grow stronger and bear more.'

'Just as you say' replied Koki.

Time went by again and the harvest came round. When Koki saw that the first ground-nuts were being lifted she went and told her husband. 'Oh, all right' said Gizo and with that he left the house and went out to a farm belonging to some Fulani. There he gathered a large calabash full of ground-nuts and with these he returned home.

'You were right, Gizo' said his wife 'these ground-nuts are very good. And strong too.'

Later on Gizo went back to the farm to make sure that there was no one about and then he invited his wife to come and see it.

'Look to the east' he said 'it's all mine as far as you can see. To the west too—all mine. And to the north and south as well.'

'All this great space' said Koki. 'You must have worked very hard, Gizo.'

When they got home again Koki said: 'Husband, this year we shall have plenty of food: you must start building cornstores so that we can keep it.'

The spider therefore built seven corn-stores and then started bringing back more ground-nuts. Each time the Fulani went to the farm and carried away what they had harvested Gizo would follow and lift what he wanted. In this way he filled four out of the seven corn-stores.

But all this time the Fulani had been asking each other who it was who was helping himself to the ground-nuts. To find out they made a doll, which they fashioned out of latex in the image of a girl, and this they placed in their farm. Then they brought dumpling stew and milk gruel and roast meat and placed it in front of the doll.

When the spider came again he saw the doll and said: 'Ah, little maid, so all this feast is yours, is it?' With that he set to and ate most of the food. When he had done he said to the doll: 'All I want now is to touch your breast and then I'll be getting along.'

So saying he stretched out a hand to touch the doll and his hand stuck fast. 'Let go, little maid' he said. 'I was only having fun.' He now stretched out the other hand and that too stuck fast. 'Let go' he said 'or I shall have to kick you'. With that he gave the doll a kick and his right foot stuck fast. 'Now this left foot of mine' he said 'has no sense of humour. Let go at once or I shall have to use it.' So saying he struck out with his left foot and that too struck fast. 'Let go' he cried 'or I shall charge you and that will hurt.' The doll didn't let go so he charged forward and his body stuck fast. 'Little maid' he cried again 'let go or I shall butt you and knock out all your teeth.' With that he tried to butt her but all that happened was that his head stuck fast.

When the Fulani returned they found the spider held fast by the doll. 'Gizo' they said 'God has delivered you up today and even if you were an elephant and not just a spider you would be in for the biggest hiding of your life.' So saying they went off into the bush to cut canes.

While they were gone the hyena appeared. 'Hullo Gizo' he said 'what are you doing here?' Then he saw the remains of the meat and asked whose it was.

'The Fulani have set me up here' said the spider 'and given me meat and stew and gruel. There's some over there which you can have if you like. I've eaten as much as I can and now they have gone off to find me a bullock. They say that it has so much meat on it that it can hardly walk.'

'I say' said the hyena 'save some for me.'

'All right' said the spider 'but you'll have to come and take my place while I go and relieve myself or when they come back they may find no one here and go away. So just come and put yourself where I am'.

'Right' said the hyena and with that he plucked the spider off the doll and took his place.

'Now mind, Kura' said the spider 'don't let me come back and find that you have eaten everything and haven't kept my share.'

'Dear me no' said the hyena. 'So long as they bring the bullock, Gizo, you'll find your share here whether you come back for it or not.'

'That's the spirit' said the spider and took himself off. When he was well clear of the farm he found a tree and climbed up into it and sat down to watch.

By and by the Fulani returned and found the hyena. 'Ah' they said 'Gizo has turned himself into a hyena. But it won't help you' they told him 'because whether you are a hyena or an elephant you're going to get the thrasing of your life.' So saying they laid into the hyena and beat him and beat him and beat him. At long last he was able to get free and run away.

After his escape the hyena happened to sit down under the tree in which the spider was sitting. 'If only I could lay my hands on that Gizo' he said to himself 'I'd eat him up, every bit, yes and drink his blood too.' At this the spider broke off a twig and let it fall to the ground. The hyena looked up and saw him and said: 'Come down and be eaten.'

'Very well' said the spider. So saying he started climbing slowly down but when he had nearly reached the ground he suddenly stopped and shouted: 'Keep away there—leave him to me.'

'Who are you talking to Gizo?' asked the hyena.

'No one much' said the spider 'just some Fulani.' This was enough for the hyena who did not wait for more but took to his heels and fled. . . .

(Hausa)

The Rabbit and the Hyena's Family

The rabbit once fell ill and when he rose from his bed of sickness he found that he had nothing to eat. While he was looking for food he came to the hyena's den where only the hyena's ten cubs were then at home. 'Peace be with you' he called out.

'Here, where do you come from?' asked the cubs.

'From outside' said the rabbit 'but Kura is my mother too.'

'What's your name then?' asked the cubs.

'I'm called All-of-us' said the rabbit.

'All right' said the cubs 'you can come in and sit down.'

The rabbit was sitting with the hyena cubs when their mother returned to the den with food. 'Is this for all of us?' asked eldest cub.

'It is' said the hyena.

'There you are' said the rabbit 'she said it was for me.' So the cubs gave up their share of the meat and the rabbit ate it all.

After a while the hyena brought more food to the den. 'Is this for all of us?' said the cubs.

'Of course it is' said the hyena.

'There you are' said the rabbit, taking it all again 'you heard what she said.'

After a while the cubs began to get thin. The hyena noticed this and said: 'Come children, step outside and let's have a look at you.' The cubs went outside and the hyena saw how thin they had grown. 'What's the matter with you?' she asked.

'Well Mother' they said 'every time you bring us food, All-of-us takes it all.'

'And who is All-of-us?' said the hyena.

'Why, he's there in the den' said the cubs.

'All-of-us' cried the hyena 'come out and let me see you.'

So the rabbit gathered up his long ears and sidled to the mouth of the den and said: 'Here I am.' The hyena was very cross indeed and seized him by those same long ears and hurled him as far as she could. As soon as he landed, he took to his heels and ran off.

The rabbit was still running away from the hyena when he met the dog. 'Here Zomo' said the dog 'where have you been lately to get so fat?'

'I've been in the hyena's den' said the rabbit.

'I say, can you show me how to get in?' asked the dog.

'Just go to the entrance' said the rabbit 'and say that your name is All-of-us.'

'Oh good' said the dog and started off. As he went along he kept saying to himself 'All-of-us, All-of-us' so that he shouldn't forget the word. But when he was near the den, he found that he had forgotten it after all and so he stopped and took counsel with himself. 'Now was it Hamizga' he asked himself 'or was it All-of-us? I'm sure that it was Hamizga.'

The dog now marched up to the hyena's den and called out 'Peace be with'.

'Where do you come from?' asked the cubs.

'Well, my name's Hamizga' said the dog 'and actually I was born outside but I was told that I could come here and live with you.'

'All right' said the cubs 'come and sit down.' So the dog went and sat down among them.

Soon afterwards the hyena appeared again. 'Mother' said the cubs 'this time we want to give our meat to Hamizga.'

'Oh?' said the hyena 'and who may Hamizga be? Let him come out so that I can see him.'

So the dog had to go out and stand before the hyena who at once sprang on him and pinned him to the ground. 'Hold him' she said to the cubs 'while I go and get some firewood and then we'll roast him and have him for supper.' But as soon as the hyena's back was turned the dog knocked down the cub who was holding him and took to his heels.

As the dog was running away from the hyena he happened to meet the rabbit again. 'So that's the way you treat me, is it?'' he said. 'Sending me to Kura's to get eaten. Well. I'm going to pay you back and eat you instead.' So saying he set off in pursuit of the rabbit.

The rabbit was running for his life with the dog after him when he happened to meet the hyena again. 'Your quarry's behind me' he cried 'catch him as he goes past.' So the hyena lay in wait for the dog and pounced on him as he came by and carried him off to his den. There the cubs ate him all up and everyone was satisfied.

(Hausa)

The Rabbit, the Elephant, and the Giraffe

The rabbit once suggested to the elephant that they should farm in partnership. 'You can clear the bush' he said 'and I'll burn the trees when you have pushed them over.' The elephant agreed and began pushing over trees to clear the land.

The rabbit next went to the giraffe and suggested to him too that they should go into farming together. 'I'll push over the trees' he said 'and you can burn them.' The giraffe agreed and went and burnt all the trees which the elephant had previously pushed over. As for the rabbit, he just took care that neither the elephant nor the giraffe knew what the other was doing.

When the first rains fell the rabbit went and found the elephant. 'Giwa' he said 'you do the sowing and I'll do the hoeing.'

Later on he went and found the giraffe. 'Rakumin Dawa' he said 'I've done the sowing and now it's your turn to do the hoeing.'

Next, when the corn was ripe, he went back to the elephant. 'Now Giwa' he said 'you go and reap and then I'll gather.'

Finally, when the elephant had done the reaping, he went back to the giraffe. 'I've finished the reaping' he said 'and now it's all ready for you to gather.'

When all the work had been done he went to see the elephant again. 'Well Giwa' he said 'the corn's all gathered so let's bring it in tomorrow. There's just one thing though' he went on 'I've heard that a creature called a giraffe is going to try to rob us of it.'

'What on earth's a giraffe?' asked the elephant. 'Well, never mind, we'll worry about that tomorrow. Off with you now.'

From the elephant the rabbit went on to the giraffe. 'I say, Rakumin Dawa' he said 'I've just heard that a creature called an elephant is going to try to rob us of our corn.'

'What on earth's an elephant?' asked the giraffe. 'Well never mind, we'll worry about that tomorrow.'

Next day the giraffe was up first and went out to the farm. When the rabbit joined him he said: 'Here Zomo, where's that elephant which you said was coming to take our corn?'

'He'll soon be here, I expect' said the rabbit. 'Look—there he is now' he added as the elephant came into sight. ''you see him?'

'Where?' said the giraffe. 'Somewhere near that hill?'

'That's not a hill' said the rabbit 'that's the elephant.'

'Good Lord!' said the giraffe. 'I can't take him on!'

'All right' said the rabbit 'if you can't, you'd better lie down here and stick your neck out.'

The giraffe did as he was told and the rabbit went over to the elephant. 'Hey Zomo' said the elephant 'where's that giraffe which you said was going to take our corn?'

'He was here early waiting for you' said the rabbit 'but he's gone to have a bathe. That's his guitar over there' he added, pointing to the outstretched neck of the giraffe.

'Good Lord!' said the elephant. 'A creature with a guitar like that is more than I can tackle.'

'All right, Diwa' said the rabbit 'if you feel you can't tackle him you'd better run for it.'

So the elephant charged off towards the east. The rabbit then went back to the giraffe and said: 'You'd better go while the going's good, Rakumin Dawa, in case he comes back and catches you.' At this the giraffe jumped up and galloped off toward the west.

So the rabbit was left with all the corn. He took it back to his house and after that he lived a life of ease.

(Hausa)

The Warrior and the Hunter and the Hunter's Wife

There was once a warrior who was the lover of the wife of a hunter. 'How can I kill him' he asked her 'so that you and I can get married?'

'Leave it to me' she replied.

Time passed and then one day the hunter's wife told the warrior to meet her at a certain place on the following Friday. On the previous evening she made her own preparations and next morning, when the hunter had gone out, she took the arrows out of his quiver, removed the arrow-heads, and replaced the shafts. Having done this she put the arrow-heads in a basket with her other things and then went off to keep her tryst with the warrior.

When the hunter returned he asked his neighbours what had become of his wife. 'We saw her take her things' they said 'and go off in a hurry.' Hearing this he dashed into his house, snatched up his bow and quiver, and set out in pursuit. After some time he caught sight of her in the distance and when he at last came up with her he found that she was already in the company of the warrior.

'On your head be it then' said the hunter to the warrior. With that he drew an arrow from his quiver and fitted it to his bow. When he saw that there was no head on the shaft, however, he cast the first arrow away and drew a second. One after another he pulled the arrows out of his quiver and fitted them to his bow but only to discover that they were all headless.

Meanwhile the warrior had tightened the girth of his saddle and mounted his horse. Now, sword in hand, he bore down upon the hunter and aimed a blow at him. The hunter, being defenceless, believed that he was done for. But at the last moment the warrior held his hand against the hunter and, wheeling round, cut down the hunter's wife instead.

"Let us be friends, you and I' he said to the hunter. 'As she could do this to you, I know that if I had killed you just now she would one day have done the same to me. Any man who gets mixed up in the affairs of women is likely to wake up and find himself dead.'

(Hausa)

Why Tortoise Is Used in Preventing Harm by Evil Spirits

Once upon a time two children went to a place called Ogodo, to the house of a chief of that place called Okolo ('one who likes excitement'). He gave them *kola* and asked their names. One of the children told him that his name was 'Heap of sense.' The other said that his name was 'Foolish child of a dunce.' The chief asked 'Heap of sense' what his name meant. He said it meant that he was very clever and could answer any difficult question whatever. The chief asked the other the meaning of his name. He said, 'It means I know nothing at all.' The chief then gave him a big hen and gave 'Heap of sense' a cock, saying, 'Take these and each of you bring me two eggs tomorrow.' Then they went home. 'Heap of sense' and Tortoise were old friends.

As the children got home the hen the chief had given Dunce laid two eggs but the cock he had given 'Heap of sense' laid nothing. 'Heap of sense' then went to find his friend and told him how they had gone to the chief's house and what he had told them to bring him. Tortoise answered, 'My friend, that is no problem. Don't go tomorrow but let Dunce go. Go yourself the following day. When the chief asks you why you didn't come on the previous day tell him that your father was in labour.' 'Heap of sense' went along in two days' time and the chief asked him why he had not come the day before. He said, 'Sir, it was because my father was in labour.' The chief exclaimed and spat in his face and said, 'Have you ever seen a man in labour?' 'Heap of sense' replied, 'Have you ever known a cock lay eggs?' The chief saw that 'Heap of sense' was certainly intelligent and said to him, 'You are to come tomorrow and pull up the great tree for me that is in front of my house.' 'Heap of sense' said he would do so and went home. He went and told Tortoise, who said there was nothing to worry about. When he arrived he should say, 'Chief, I beg you to chew this stone which is in front of the compound and spray it out on my chest, to give me strength to pull up the tree at once.' 'Heap of sense' went back and said this to the chief, who scolded him and said, 'Have you ever seen anyone who chewed a stone?' 'Heap of sense' retorted, 'Have you ever seen anyone who pulled up a tree as big as this one with his hands?' The chief considered what to do and then said, 'You are to drink up all the water in the sea tomorrow.' 'Heap of sense' then went home and again told his friend Tortoise, who said, 'That is easy. When you arrive dip one finger into the sea, lick it and tell the chief it is not salt enough and you are not going to eat anything which hasn't got enough salt.' The child went and told the chief this, who said, 'Didn't you know that the sea wasn't salt enough?' 'Heap of sense' replied, 'Have you ever seen anyone who could drink up all the water in the sea?'

The chief was astonished at the child's answers and said to him, 'I wish you to bring me whoever it is that teaches you all these things.' 'Heap of sense' went home and told Tortoise, who agreed to come, thinking that the chief would give him some present. They went to the chief's house, where he gave them *kola*, picked up Tortoise and put medicine in incisions in his face and said, 'Tortoise, you will always be used to render harmless (cover) evil spirits and to drive away wicked people who trouble us. You will be used in divining and your shell will be used to give sense and intelligence to those who lack them, to make them sensible. Go away now and in the evening we will take you for this work.' As Tortoise was going he said, 'Guardian spirit of the land, let me not be used to obliterate evil spirits.' The medicine the chief had put into the cuts in his face answered him, 'You must be used to obliterate evil spirits.' He went and hid in a ditch, but the chief came and asked about him and the medicine told him that Tortoise was in the ditch. The chief said to the medicine,

'Bring Tortoise to me.' The medicine lifted Tortoise out of the ditch. Tortoise was used to obstruct evil spirits and wicked people in that chief's land.

Since that time, therefore, Tortoise is always used in divining, and in giving stupid people some sense. He is also used in covering up bad medicine in Igbo land, and in seizing evil spirits and bad people if they give trouble.

(Igbo, Nigeria)

The Story of the Four Miracle Workers

There was a man whose wife bore him a son. He called his name Musavili. But he was a very arrogant and stubborn boy. Sometimes he refused to eat his food, and when his mother bought him new clothes he refused to wear them, saying that they were rubbish.

One day he said, 'Mother, go and buy me a flask and a hat. I want to leave home and go away for ever.' So the mother bought him a flask, and a very expensive hat worth eighty shillings. When she gave them to him, he threw them away, and said they were useless. His mother was disgusted, and she said to him, 'Go where you want to go!' Then he left his home and began to wander about in the forests.

One day, when he was walking in the plains, he saw a man from a long distance. As he went nearer, he noticed that the man was kneeling down, and had a gun in his hands. He said to the man, 'Please do not shoot me.' The boy came to him, and greeted him, 'How do you do?' He replied, 'How do you do, Musavili?' The boy was surprised to find that the man knew his name, and he said to him, 'So you know my name?'

'Yes, I do,' answered the man.

'And what are you doing here?' the boy inquired.

'I am waiting until some flies alight on top of Mount Kilimanjaro, so I can shoot them!'

'How can you see a fly on top of such a high mountain?'

The man gave him power to see that far, and said to the boy, 'Now watch it.' He looked and saw a fly alight on the snow-capped peak, and the man with the gun shot and broke its wing. Then he said to the boy, 'Would you like to join me in my travel?'

'Yes, very much so,' answered the boy joyfully.

The man said, 'Very well. Let us be going then.' So they went together. They travelled until the man said to the boy, 'Can you see that man over there?' He answered, 'Yes, I can. But he seems to be standing on one leg only.' The man said, 'Let us get where he is.' They walked on until they came to the man standing on one leg. They greeted him, 'How do you do?' He replied, 'How do you do, Musavili and your friend?'

Musavili asked him, 'Why are you standing on one leg only?'

The man answered, 'If I should step on the ground with my other leg, I would quickly move from here to another spot immediately.' Musavili said, 'Try it and let us see.' The man stepped on both feet, and no sooner did he do that than he moved very fast and got back to the home of Musavili. It had taken the boy two years to travel all that distance, but this man did it within no time. The man came back and said to Musavili, 'If you want to, you may join me in my travel.' Musavili said he would. The man said, 'Good. Let us be going then.'

When they had travelled a few more miles, this new man said to Musavili, 'Do you see that person yonder there?' The boy looked and said, 'Yes, I do. He looks like a man, but he seems to be holding his nose.' The two men said, 'Let us get where he is.' So they all went on until they reached the man who was blocking his nostrils with a hand. They greeted him, saying, 'How do you do?' He replied, 'How do you do, Musavili and your two friends?' Then Musavili asked him, 'Why have you blocked your nostrils with your hand?' The man replied, 'If I open my nostrils there will be a very strong wind!' Musavili said, 'Open them a little bit and let us see what happens.' The man did so, and suddenly a very strong wind began to blow, knocked down all the trees around where they were. Musavili immediately said to him, 'Please close your nostrils again.' When he closed them the wind stopped blowing, and the man said to Musavili, 'You may join me, if you want.' They all travelled together, and then they saw another man holding his wallet. Musavili was asked, 'Can you see that man?' He answered, 'Yes, but he seems to be uprooting all the large trees and squeezing them into his small wallet. So they came to where this other man was, and greeted him, 'How do you do, man?' And he replied, 'How do you do Musavili and your three friends?'

"What is your name?' Musavili asked him.

'My name is Mukua-miamba. The name means "one who uproots *baobab* trees".'

'Will you uproot a few so we can see.'

He said, 'I have uprooted very many, and I have also uprooted hills. Wait one moment, I will show them to you.' Then he pulled out of his little wallet, one hill after another. The man said to Musavili, 'You may join me if you want.' Musavili said to Mukua-miamba, 'Yes, I will join you.' The man replied, 'Very well, come, and let us be going.'

They went on until they came to the palace of the king of that country. They were welcomed, and given beds to sleep on. The following day there was a horse race at the palace, and thousands of his subjects came to take part and to watch. The king said that the winner would be given his beautiful daughter to be his wife. The group that Musavili had joined was asked, 'Is there anyone among you who can take part in these competitions?' Musavili answered, 'We shall try to find someone.' All those that come to compete brought their own horses, and so a horse was produced by the king, for Musavili and his group. But Musavili told the king that although one of them was going to take part, he would not use a horse but would merely run. The judges said, 'Are you merely taking it as a joke?' Musavili answered, 'No, we are serious.' The judges said, 'It is up to you.'

The whistle was blown, and the competitors began to run. After three hours, the man who walked on one leg decided now to run. He lowered his other leg and ran as fast as lightning. He reached the river, passing the other competitors on the way, and then turned to go back. But because he was so far ahead of the others, he stopped on the way back, and lay down and went to sleep. The king's daughter came, together with the other people, and they took his pitcher while he slept, and spilled all his water, and ran back to the palace. The other competitors now reached the river, and filled their pitchers, and began to gallop back to the palace.

The people waited anxiously at the palace, and began to ask one another, 'When will the winner get here?' Musavili heard it, and got very concerned. He asked the man who was shooting flies to look and find him, and when he did, Musavili asked him to shoot on his ear in order to wake him up. So the man was gently shot, and he woke up, only to find that his water had been spilled. Immediately he put down his other leg, got to the river again, filled up the pitcher and within two minutes he reached the palace. He passed all the other competitors on the way, and he became the winner. Everyone clapped his hands and congratulated him. When the other runners arrived, they were astonished to find him already there.

The king said to Musavili and his people, 'Tomorrow you will be given my daughter.' So they went to sleep, and at night, Musavili and the other men said to Mukua-miamba, 'Remove the house in which the princess is sleeping, and put it into your little wallet, and let us all go away. Remove the king's palace as well, and let us put it into the sea.' So the palace was removed and put into the sea, and both the king and his daughter and all those in the palace perished.

In the morning Musavili and his men saw about 30,000 soldiers following them, carrying guns. So they said to the man who kept his nostrils blocked, 'It is your turn now.' The man answered, 'Stand aside and see what happens.' So he opened his nostrils, and a very strong wind blew off all those soldiers into the sea, and they also drowned and perished.

These four men went with Musavili till they reached his home country, and they became kings. They are still ruling to this day.

(Kamba, Kenya)

The Hare and His Wisdom

All the beasts once lived in a village of Konu. The most powerful ones, the Elephant, Hippo, and Lion oftentimes fought with one another. This was so because each wanted to become a great leader.

Thus they entered into a campaign. Each promised the small and weak better living conditions and reform in the rules governing conduct in Konu.

In those days there were some places where animals such as the rabbit, squirrel, impala, goat, cow and other animals with little strength were not allowed to go. And from the great lake, the weaker animals were allowed but two sips of water, twice a day. The best regions were reserved for the powerful beasts of the forest.

When all the animals of Konu had gathered, the campaign began.

The Lion's promise was this: he would allow everyone to graze anywhere they wished. They could also drink from the lake at any time. The Lion said, 'The Elephant does not allow you to drink too much water for fear that there will be none left for him. The Hippo supports him, saying if the lake goes dry the Hippo will have no place to live. The best pastures are used by the Elephant and the Hippo. You must graze a distance away on dry acres where grass is sparse. Futher-more, the Elephant and the Hippo show they care little for the small animals. They step on the squirrel, or the rat, and show little sorrow.'

The other animals knew that the Lion spoke the truth. They were ready to give their votes for Kingship to the Lion.

Then the Elephant made his speech 'I declare that I will take the utmost caution in the future to see that no smaller animals are crushed by my foot. But I have only killed by accident, never by design as has the Lion. If the Lion becomes King, you will be his victims. Remember that the Lion does not eat grass or leaves; he eats meat. Is it better for you to drink much water, eat all the rich green grass you want, and later make a fat meal for the Lion? Or is it better to drink less water, eat regular grass, and live as long as one's life span permits.?'

The audience was stirred by the words of the Elephant. They shouted with happiness, and said the Elephant must be their King. It now seemed decided.

The Hippo stood up and said, 'Friends, give your attention to me!'

Some of the animals, who knew what a treacherous beast the Hippo could be, shouted, 'No, no! Do not listen to him.'

The Hippo stood firm and waited for silence. In a voice falsely innocent, he said, 'Have I not been kind in the past? The only reason I have guarded the lake is so that all the animals will have water in time of drought.'

The audience muttered. More than one animal doubted the truth of the Hippo's words.

The Hippo lost patience and shouted, 'The lake belongs to me! Therefore if I do not become King of Konu, nobody will drink. This includes the Lion and the Elephant. I will have Crocodiles guard the beaches and carry out my law.'

It appeared to the weaker animals that they must bow to the power of the Hippo; fear of him would make him King. And yet, the Elephant had spoken strongly.

Among the crowd listening to the Powerful Ones and their debate was a small Hare. He knew that the animals would not vote for the Lion. The Lion and his appetite were the greater evil. But how would they choose? Would it be the Elephant or the Hippo? The Hare himself had wanted the Kingship. Would anyone listen to such as he?

The Hare gathered courage and rose up, saying, 'I have a plan that may help us choose a King.'

Some, like the Zebra and the Horse, laughed at the lowly Hare.

When he had been given their attention, the Hare said, 'It should be decided by a tug-of-war. I offer myself as opponent to the Eelephant, and then to the Hippo. I will face them alone, and must have all the area cleared of animals, save these two Powerful Ones.'

The Zebra snorted, 'What good is this? Both the Elephant and the Hippo could easily pull a Hare.'

The Horse said, At least one of us Lesser Ones shows bravery.'

And all the animals agreed that there must be some way to decide the Kingship. The Hippo, and the Elephant also, said they would meet the Hare in a tug-of-war.

On the morrow, the Hare went to the Elephant with one end of a long rope. He said. 'Stand here. When I whistle, begin to pull.'

The Hare took the other end of the long rope to the Hippo. He said, 'Stand here. When I whistle, begin to pull.'

The Hare stood at the halfway mark. He whistled. The Elephant and the Hippo each pulled for one hour, until all their strength was gone.

The Hare raced to the Elephant and said, 'You have lost the tug-of-war.'

The Hare raced to the Hippo and said, 'You have lost the tug-of-war.'

Each was ashamed because he thought he had lost to the lowly Hare. So both said to him, 'You are the strongest. You should be the King.'

All the animals of Konu gathered to hear the result. They whispered to one another, 'If the Elephant is King, then the Hippo will not allow us water. But if the Hippo is King, the Elephant might not let us have any pasture.'

Then slowly the Hare rose up to speak to the crowd. 'To my pleasure, I wish to tell you that neither Elephant nor Hippo is our King. The very lowly person you see here has proved his strength by defeating two of the most powerful beasts of the forest.'

Thus the Hare became King of the beasts of Konu. He had not defeated them by great muscles; rather he had outwitted them. The lowly Hare was a good King. His strength was the strength of wisdom, rather than the strength of a powerful body.

(Kenya)

Nyamgondho Son of Ombare

There once lived an old man alone in a small hut on an isolated hillside facing western shores. Nyamgondho Ombare was a fisherman. So devoted was he to his occupation he hardly stayed away from his fishing nets and his beautiful canoe. He would spend many hours mending fishing nets. Occasionally he took a nap under the shade of a big euphobia tree. Or he would simply sit straight with his back to it, thinking about the lake and his experience with it.

Nyamgondho was a poor man; he had no wife, and apart from his fishing nets and his canoe his other possessions were a cow, a goat, and a hen. Despite his poverty he was a good-natured man who never held any grudge against anyone. He never blamed anyone for his condition. For him it was all due to fate. He was never jealous of those who were rich even though he knew they did not care about him. He usually went around smiling, praying and hoping that his grand relatives' spirits might someday reward him.

Nyamgondho had yet another quality—he liked children and was good with them. He liked them for definite reasons. He knew that it is only in early childhood that a person is a person for his own sake. Children never laughed at him. He would share the very little he had with them; he would play with them, take them swimming or even take them for a cruise in his canoe. Being poor for Nyamgondho was not something to be shamed of.

Although he had great interest in the lake, his luck was not altogether great. He cast his nets every evening, but each morning when he hauled them in to his disappointment, there were no fish to speak of. If he came home with a catch of more than two, it was his greatest luck.

But one morning something happened. Instead of catching fish, his nets brought to him a woman out of the lake. He was frightened, but, after he almost let her go back into the water, she assured him that it was all right. As he rowed to shore yet another strange thing happened. This time there was a whole herd of cattle, goats, sheep and poultry following behind them. It was too good for him to believe. Within a day Nyamgondho became the richest of all the people in his clan. He had everything he wanted now including a wife. He caught so many fish that his small canoe could not bring them ashore on one trip. He was happy and relaxed, and he thanked his ancestors for listening to his prayers.

But one day he was invited to take part in a clan ritual. He and his wife went. There was much drinking. In fact, people drank till the next morning. Nyamgondho got so drunk that he even went so far as to scold other people, telling them how rich he was and how they should not say anything in his presence. When his wife told him to keep quiet, he hit her and called her names. The next morning his wife packed up and started for the lake. As she took off, everything that she came with went with her—cattle, goats, sheep, etc. Nyamgondho tried to beg her to stay; he apologized for his misdemeanors, but she would not listen. Nyamgondho could do nothing but watch her go back to the lake. He could not move. He is still standing there.

(Note: It is commonly believed that Nyamgondho is still standing by the lake but in the form of a rock. This version is by Henry Olela.)

(Kenya)

Six Nyanga Texts

1

Two men went to trap in the forest. While they were trapping, one of them killed a young wild pig. They went to the village; said to one another, 'If we lay this young pig aside (which is our first kill), then our traps will fail to kill; and so the headman and others will they not hear about that in the village?' The other one, he also said to his companion, 'When we have finished eating this small pig there in the forest, the teeth of the pig cannot be hidden, will the village headman not hear?' They came to a decision to eat the young pig. They said, 'As we are here, both of us, there is no one who will take the news to the village, so our traps will not become "not-killing anything."' They took the small pig, cut it into pieces: the two men shared it. After they had set their traps again and had finished eating the animal they went up to the village.

Two days passed; they are in the village. One of them got up (early) to sit round the fire in the men's hut, where his companions are. He was giving other news, and there they are, laughing, while sitting round the fire. And he who has remained in the house sleeping, he got up and went to the place where his companion is. He arrived there; they are laughing. He said to his companion, 'You, what news are you telling here, not that of the small pig we ate in the forest?' All his companions said to him, 'Look! you have eaten a young pig in the forest!' His companion told him, 'You are shaming yourself, for I have been telling other news and there you are appearing and revealing (the secret of) the small pig, saying that we have hidden it and have eaten it in the forest.'

All the men, together with the headman, finished hearing this news of the hidden thing.

2

There was a man; he had begotten seven children. Their names were Yangara, all of them together, all had this same name and their father also was Yangara. Yangara said to his children: 'Because you quarrel with one another about this name Yangara, you all go to the forest to kill a buffalo, then you will be able to take the name of Yangara.'

All these, all together they went to the forest. They went to run across the buffaloes' path. The elder (brother) asked his brothers saying, 'What are we going to do?' The one who follows at his back said to their elder, 'You will know how we will act, you will find the teaching that will make known to us (how) to kill this buffalo, because you are Yangara as my father is also. The elder set his foot on the ground: dug out a trench. And the one who follows him said to him, 'You have not covered the ditch.' The third one said to them, 'Your brainpower is useless'; he took a leaf, covered (the trench) with it there. After some days had passed, there died in this ditch a buffalo. The fourth Yangara tied it up; took it out. In order to carry it, Yangara the fourth took a knife, and cut the animal; cut it into pieces, just pieces. The fifth one wrapped it; wrapped it up, and carried it to the village: he too was up to that knowledge. Also the sixth one carried it on his back, laid it down at his father's; he also was Yangara. Their father inquired about all their knowledge: to dig, to cover, to take the animal out of the trench, to carry it, to cut it into pieces, to wrap it up in bundles.

Their younger (brother) remained behind (i.e. was left) among them, the last-born, he sought a piece of wood and beat it saying, 'He who has died may he rise again!' The Buffalo stood up, went his way to the forest from where it had come. This child told his father, saying that he had sent the buffalo back to the forest because it was (too) small to share out to all the people; therefore he found out how to send it back. His father said to him, 'You also have not done wrong.' All of them he called by the name Yangara.

3

There was a man; he begot a boy. This man became sick of an illness. When he was about to die, he asked his child, saying, 'When I will have finished dying, what will you do?' He said to him that he did not know. He said to him, 'When he dies you will cut off the little finger, that little finger will save you; when he has finished dying, that little finger you will put it near the door, you will dig it in there.' Then his father died; he cut off his finger, and dug out a grave in the middle of the village ground.

When a month had passed after his father had died, he woke up early, saw in the village houses had grown up like crops around where he was. He became chief; all the inhabitants were bringing him tribute.

While they were sitting thus with joy, his wife questioned him. And there where the finger had been dug in, there was sprouting a *musae*-tree. She asked her husband saying, 'We were poor and now we are rich, from where does it come our richness?' When she got tired with her husband, he went to tell her about the secret counsel which had been left to him by his father, what he had been asked to do and how he had put that little finger in the grave. When his wife had heard this news—just imagine, she was being adulterous with a man—she gave the news to her lover, all the news, what her husband had done and why he had become chief.

In the early morning he assembled all his people; they came, asked him why his tree was staying here, that such a tree was not in the middle of the village. He failed to give them a reply, he said that this tree was self-grown. She appeared there, his sweetheart, his wife, revealed everything of how this tree had grown. This chief lost his chief's status.

4

There was a woman, she gives birth to two children; the first-born is Bureo and the other one is Murero. Their mother is Nyabureo.

His mother said to Bureo as she was going to the forest, 'When you see the child is crying, cook him dry bananas.' After his mother had gone to the forest, there, where Bureo has remained, the child begins to cry. He took it, killed it, cooked it with the dry bananas, saying his mother had told him when the child begins crying to cook it with bananas. He cooked it, having finished killing him. His mother came back, asked Bureo, saying, 'Where is your younger brother?' He replied that she had said to him that when the child cries he should cook it with bananas; he had finished cooking it.

His mother, when she saw that she does not see her child, sang:

> 'Bureo, stupid fellow (lit. 'Father', 'venereal disease'),
> Has eaten my child.
> Catch for me Bureo
> He has eaten my child
> Catch for me Bureo
> He has eaten it with bananas
> Catch for me Bureo'

While she was chasing him here and there (to and fro) to kill him, he escaped.

There where he escaped, he met women from God's place (*il rencontra des femmes de chez Dieu*); they showed him the way. There where he went he met tree-clearers felling trees. They said to him, 'What are you fleeing for?' He said to them that he was fleeing from the women who say that he had revealed their secret and that the secret of women is not to be disclosed.

There where his mother was left, she sang:

> 'Catch for me Bureo,
> He has eaten my child
> He has eaten it with bananas.'

He passed beyond the tree-clearers; he came out near the river there where water is drawn. He met his paternal aunt (lit. 'female father'); his paternal aunt drew water after she had put Bureo in the jar. When she had arrived at (the house of) Kirimu (Monster), her husband the Monster Shebeni Muesa told his wife to give him water; she gave it to him. When he had tasted from it, he said that the water smelt like man. The Monster drank the water of another jar. After he had finished drinking that water, he got up (to go). This paternal aunt took the child away, put it on a heap of dirt, showed him the road that is leading to his maternal uncles, the Bats. There where he had gone to his maternal uncles, they took Bureo, forged him, sang:

> 'Bureo has refused the forge
> The forge is this one
> I am forging the sororal nephew
> The forge is this one.'

After they had finished forging him, the wanderer went, being called by the Monster Shebeni Muesa. He turned up at (the house of) the Monster. This one said to him that there, at his house, no other man arrives who is shaved with a razor. He told him, 'Let us go to Misukuubira, where comes out the dew of fire.' There they meet early, to fight with one another, to rush headlong one against the other. Bureo told him, 'We will go to Misukuubira when we have finished gambling.' He sang:

> 'He is gambling with Monster
> May his gambling beat him!'

They cast the dice (shells) one on the other; Bureo hit all the Monster's things. After he had been completely beaten, he told the child: that they should go to Misukuubira, both of them.

They set out to there, the child sang, 'We go with Shebeni to Misukuubira.'

They arrived there; Shebeni Muesa died there.

The child returned with the trophy of the Monster to show its paternal aunt that Shebeni Muesa is dead.

This Burco went with fame; he was strong in the village of Monster Shebeni Muesa.

5

Sun and Rain started an argument with one another.

A young Monkey had begotten a daughter in another village. Rain arrived there, looking for this young girl. After he had arrived there, he talked to Monkey about his daughter. The father of the girl refused. After Rain has received this answer, he returned without anything and covered with shame.

When Sun had seen that Rain failed to get the girl, he, Sun, arrived there, asked for the girl, got her, and so became son-in-law of Monkey. War (danger) arrived, pursued Monkey. This war killed Monkey's wife and all his children, and he also had finished fleeing. There, where Monkey had fled, he shouted, 'You, Sun, because of the way you shone therefore I lose a lot of people.'

One day again, they hunted and hunted at Monkey's place. Rain also fell. They left him above, he had finished climbing up into the trees. Rain did not stop, it fell very hard. The hunters went home because of too much rain. After Rain has finished falling and Monkey has been saved, he (Rain) came to where he was and told him, 'You have given your daughter to Sun, saying he can save you, but I here have saved you and this although you have denied me your daughter.'

After he had thus been saved by Rain, Monkey took away his daughter from Sun, gave her to Rain because he had saved him. Rain went home with the daughter of Monkey where before he had been refusing her. His strength and his strong intelligence, it is because of that he got her.

6

Isimbasimba and Ntanga made blood-brotherhood. Both are with their fathers and their mothers, together, all of them. One day, Ntanga's father became ill. Isimbasimba told his friend, 'Medicine can cure your father, it is good to search for the bark of a *musoke*-tree, you will tie it fast to the belly; it's like a belt that you will tie around your father's belly, but strong people should tie it, not people who have no strength.' He took the bark of a *musoke*-tree, fastened it to the belly firmly, saying, 'As long as your father has not recovered, you will not remove this belt from around his belly.'

Days have passed; his father was cured. When they saw his father had completely recovered they untied the belt. Ntanga's body went up, then sank down, in the middle there remained nothing. Ntanga had said much wrong about his friend, saying his friend had made him pass through amazing things so that he becomes a cripple.

When days have passed, Isimbasimba's father became ill; he sent a messenger to Ntanga. He asked him to show him a medicine, as his father had become ill. Ntanga arrived at the end of the village; they are beginning to weep as the father of his companion is already dead. He says, go, first, and bite on a small piece of wood that he may die leaving to you a good word. He went to bite on a small piece of wood:

Ntanga said, 'Bite hard; hold on strongly, don't let it go.' Isimbasimba, his father died, and he is still (busy) on that small piece of wood; there where he bit on it he also died there.

These two men outdid one another in amazing things in this way.

(Republic of Zaire)

Onecike

There was a man who had a child; when he had had this child and he had reached the age of about seven, his mother died. When his mother died, the child was left alone with his father. After he had lived with him for some time, his father also died. The child was left homeless and alone; there was no one in his father's family and no one in his mother's family, nor even any friend of his father's to take care of him. So the child was alone, and as yet was not strong enough to fend for himself. He began to have many jiggers; he had some in his feet, and even right up to his knees. His body was covered with scabies and his head with ringworm. He found it difficult to get any food. After thinking things over for a long time, Onecike [1] felt he could not remain like this any longer, and said to himself, 'Let us go and find a protector. But where? And if anyone tries to harm me, what will be, will be.'

Onecike set off at random. He walked a very long time and suddenly heard the noise of a smithy. He said to himself, 'Maybe there is someone there.'

Onecike went to the place where the noise was coming from. He came near the smithy and found the smith at work.

He entered the shed and sat down. 'Smith,' he said, 'I have come to you because I want to blow the bellows in your smithy.' The smith replied, 'That is all right with me.' The smith adopted the child and entrusted him to his senior wife. Onecike was first of all given the bellows to blow, and in return the smith took him under his care. The child's health improved, although he was only given *ma* [2] crusts to eat.

Onecike said to the smith, 'Mbapa, [3] make me a fish-hook so that I can go to the river to catch some fish.' The smith made him a fish-hook and gave it to him. Onecike got his fishing-rod ready, and one day went to fish in the river and caught many fish. Onecike came back to the village with the fish, went to the woman to whom he had been entrusted and gave them to her. The woman took the fish and prepared them. Having cooked them, all she put by for him was the heads and some *ma* crusts. Onecike took this food, but when he saw it he was disappointed and exclaimed, 'Now I brought this fish, and I am only getting the heads. But what can I do about it?' Onecike ate the *ma* crusts and the fish-heads.

Another day Onecike went fishing again, and caught even more fish than the first time. He brought the fish back to the village and gave it to his adoptive mother. She prepared it and once again gave him fish-heads and *ma* crusts. Onecike's heart overflowed with bitterness.

Another day, on his way to fish he was grumbling and saying to himself, 'Here I am, going off again for nothing, for of the fish I bring back each time they only leave me the heads, while the others eat the tasty part.' He came near the river, took his hook and threw it in the water, and pulled out a fish. Onecike threw in his hook again and this time it remained caught on a tree trunk. However hard he pulled, the hook did not come off. Onecike said to himself, 'Maybe it is a fish holding back my hook.' But no, it was indeed a tree trunk the hook was caught on. He said, 'Now that hook is lost, how shall I dare go back to my master?' He pondered, 'If I am to be the victim of the wild beasts which infest the waters, so be it, for I cannot leave someone else's fish-hook in the water and go back empty-handed to a village where I am only a stranger.' He dived in and swam along the fish-line to where the hook was caught.

When he got to the bottom of the water, he was very surprised to find himself in a very crowded village. He saw in front of him his father and mother who had died long ago, and were now welcoming him warmly. The whole village was celebrating. They walked on ahead of Onecike and showed him to a house that was amply stocked with wealth of all kinds; in that house there was a large number of rooms.

His parents showed Onecike a door which they forbade him to open so long as he lived in that house. They said to him, 'You can enter every room, all their riches will be yours, but do not cross the threshold of the forbidden door.' Onecike agreed. In the underground village (actually under the river-bed) there was soon no one who recognized him as the poor little orphan. He lived in plenty and only dressed in fine clothes. He was living in a chief's big village. He lived there many years, but finally was seized with dissatisfaction.

One evening he said, 'Now I am rich, I am living in a big village, where I am staying with my father and mother who died long ago, yet I am forever haunted by the longing to open the door of that little room. I cannot resist much longer; I shall end by opening that room, and nothing will happen when I do.'

One day when these same thoughts were troubling him he went to the room and opened the door. When he had entered, far from finding himself in the room he had imagined, he was carried back to the moment when his fish-hook had been caught on the tree-trunk. Once again he was dressed in rags, and covered with scabies, ringworm, and jiggers. All these misfortunes which had left him in the underground village where he was with his father and mother, all befell him again. Onecike at the river's edge looked in vain about him for the big, populous village, the big house, the wealth and the belongings he had enjoyed. 'What a plight I am in; I can no longer go back to the village I left such a long time ago.' The hook was still firmly caught on the tree. He said to himself, 'There is nothing for it but to dive back into the water and go back there.' He dived in and disappeared, and never again reached the world of his ancestors.

You see how a fool lost his happiness because he wanted to see what should have remained hidden from him.

So ends my story.

[1] 'Onecike' = 'orphan, homeless child.'
[2] 'Ma' = food made with rice or millet.
[3] 'Mbapa, mpapa' = form of address for certain male relatives and other adults.

(Central Zaire)

Proverbs and Aphorisms

Ba rikid akura ke da wuya ba, a yi wutsiya.
It's not changing into a hyena that's difficult—it's finding a tail, i.e.
   it is often the little things which are the hardest.

Kowa ya daure kura, ya san yanda zai yi ya kwance ta.

Whoever catches a hyena should know how he's going to release it,
    i.e. you should know how an enterprise will end before you under-
    take it.

Wukar fidar giwa ba girma gareta ba sai dai kaifi.
The knife for flaying an elephant doesn't have to be large, only sharp.

Alhaki kare ne, mai-shi ya ke bi.
Guilt is a dog which follows its master.

Ko da zaki ya zama wulakantacce, ba ya yi wasa da hinziri ba.
Even if the lion comes down in the world he doesn't consort with the
    pig.

Ran wanka ba a boyon cibi.
On bath day there's no hiding the navel.

Baki shi ya kan yanka wuya.
It's the tongue that cuts the throat, i.e. talking too much gets a man
    into trouble.

Labarin zuciya a tambayi fuska.
For news of the heart ask the face, i.e. a man's character shows in his
    face.

A bar kaza cikin gashinta.
Leave the fowl in its feathers, i.e. let well alone.

Mai-ido-daya ba ya gode Allah sai ya ga makafo.
The one-eyed man doesn't thank God until he sees a man who is blind.

Kome na duniya, wani 'na gaba da wani.
All the world has its peck-order.

Laifin dadi karewa.
Pleasure's fault is that it comes to an end.

Kome ka ke takama a duniya, wani ya fi ka.
Pride yourself on what you will, someone in the world excels you.

Magana zarar bunu in ta fita ba a mayarwa.
A word once spoken is like a straw pulled from the thatch: there's no
    putting it back.

Kowa ya gaya maka rowa ya so abinka ne.
Whoever calls you a skinflint wants something from you.

Da arziki da hassada tare su ke kwana.
Envy is the bedfellow of wealth.

Laifi tudu ne, kowaya hau nasa, ya fadi na wani.
Faults are like hills: every man mounts his own and proclaims an-
    other's.

Kada a nemi kyau ga matar hamsa, sai dai ta yi miya mai-zaki.
Don't look for beauty in a cheaply bought wife: be thankful if she can
    make good relish.

Da mugun rawa gara kin tashi.
If you can't dance well, better not take the floor at all.

In ka ji ganga 'na amo, za ta fashe ne.
When a drum sounds loud it's about to burst.

(Hausa aud Fulani)

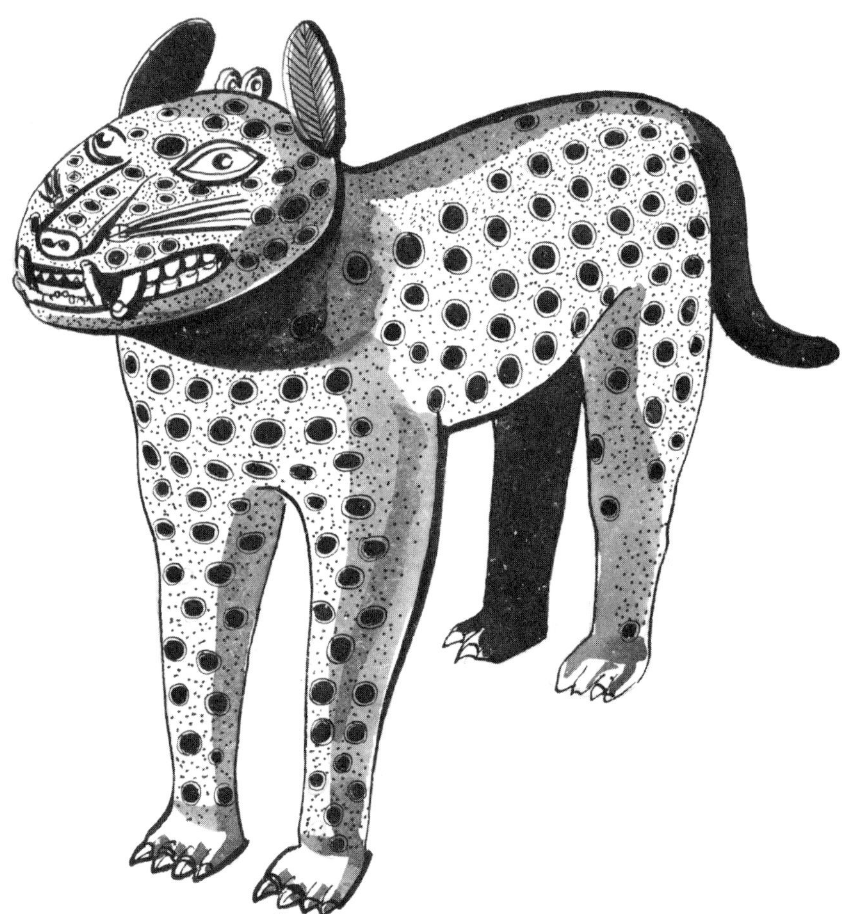

Fig. 12. Benin leopard. Bronze over clay. Approximately life-size. Nigeria, 17th century. A decorative symbol of power in the Oba's palace in ancient Benin where live leopards were used both as guards and pets. Some of these figures were hollowed-out and used to hold sacred water for ceremonial purposes; these were called "aquamanile."

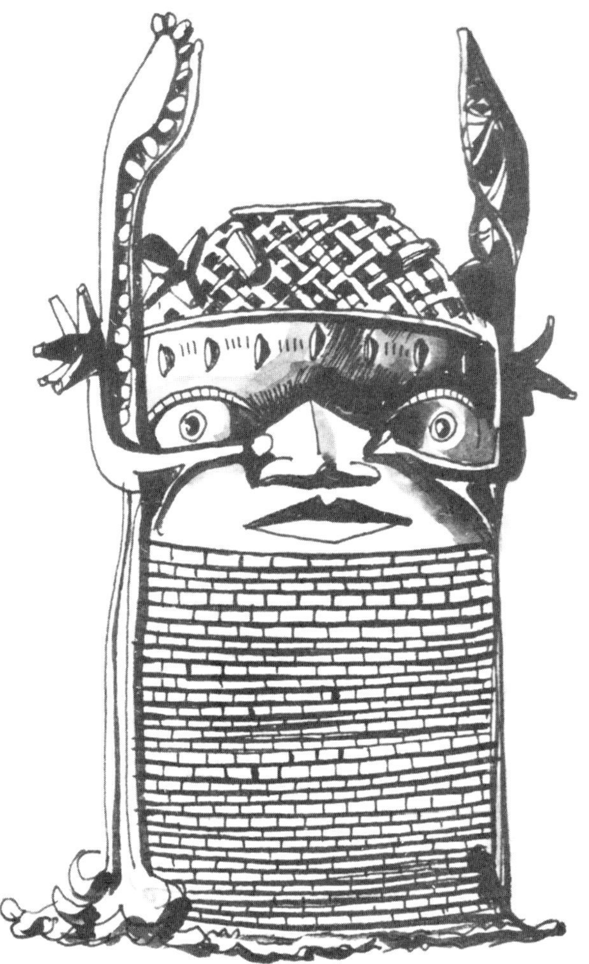

Fig. 13. An Oba (Ruler) of Benin. Bronze over clay. Nigeria. Approximately early 19th century. Height approximately 20 inches. Note the heavy ornamentation and the characteristic high collar of coral denoting royality, power and strength. Originally the figure probably supported the tusk of an elephant, also elaborately carved. Now in the British Museum.

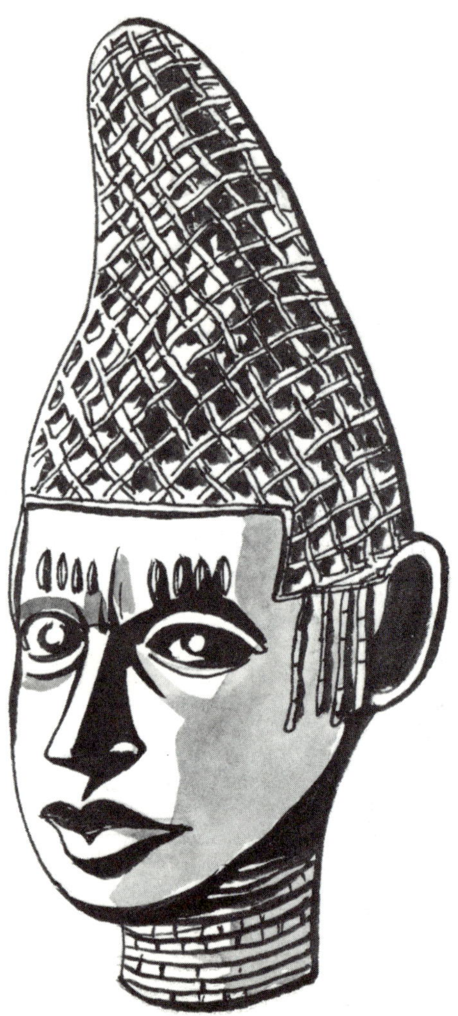

Fig. 14. Queen Mother of Benin. Bronze over clay. Life-size. Nigeria. Approximately 19th century. One of several royal portraits with characteristic basketweave headdress, high coral collar and a serenely regal expression.

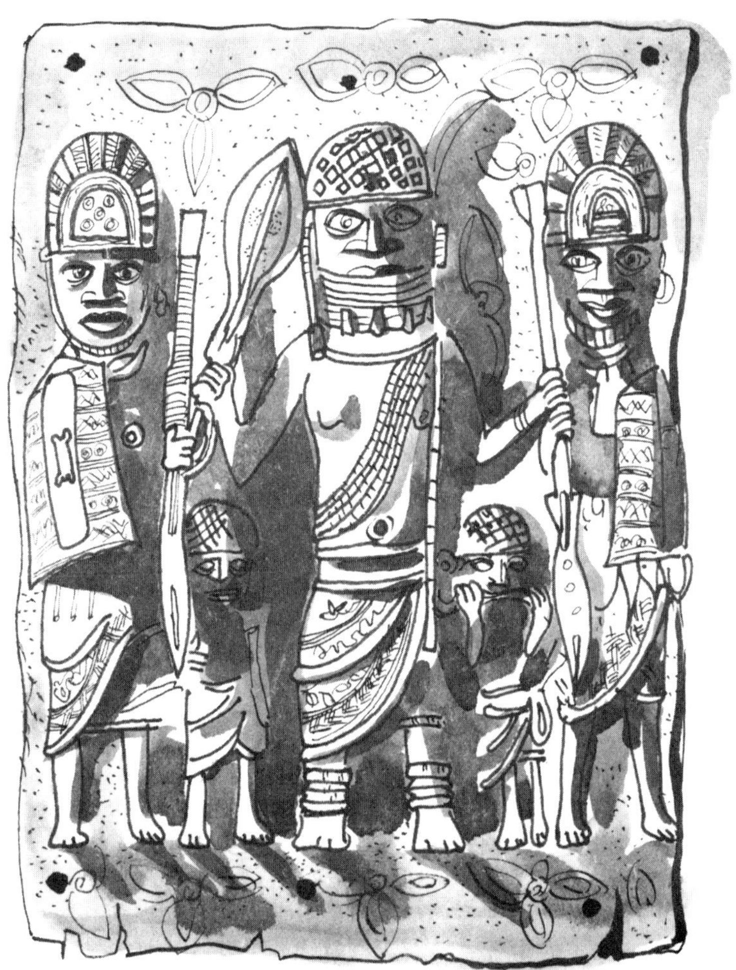

Fig. 15. Royal Benin figure, warriors and servants. Bronze over clay plaque. Approximately 18½ inches in height. 18th century. Nigeria. Note the two-edged ceremonial sword, the coral crown, necklace and anklets; also note the characteristically foreshortened legs in contrast to the enlarged head and torso. The small servants may have been pygmy captives or reduced in size to show inferior status.

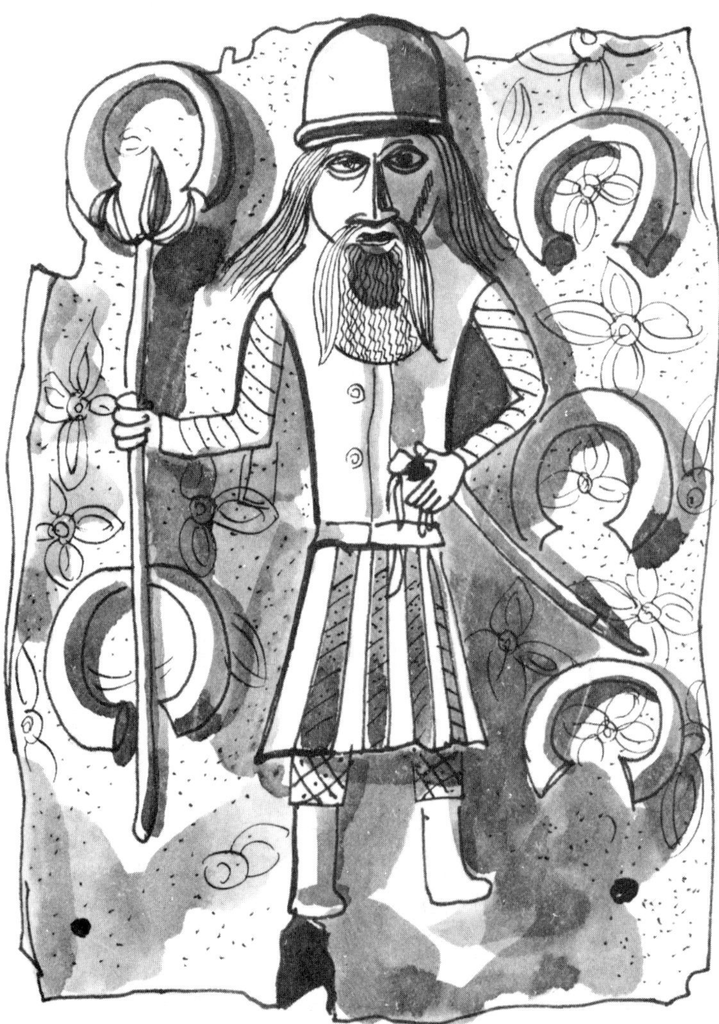

Fig. 16. Portrait of a Portuguese with staff of office. Bronze over clay plaque. Height 18½ inches. Benin, Nigeria. Middle period, approximately 18th century. Now in Vienna Museum.

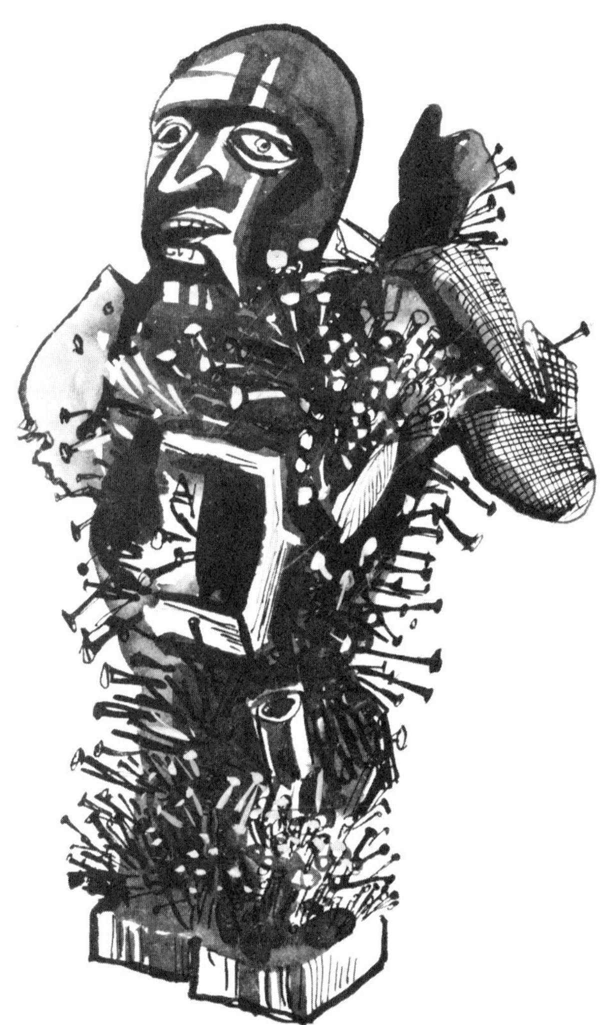

Fig. 17. Nail fetish. Wood studded with nails and spikes. Height approximately 4 inches. Zaire. The sharp objects were probably driven in to draw out the "power" contained within rather than to inflict punishment or to harm any person the image represented.

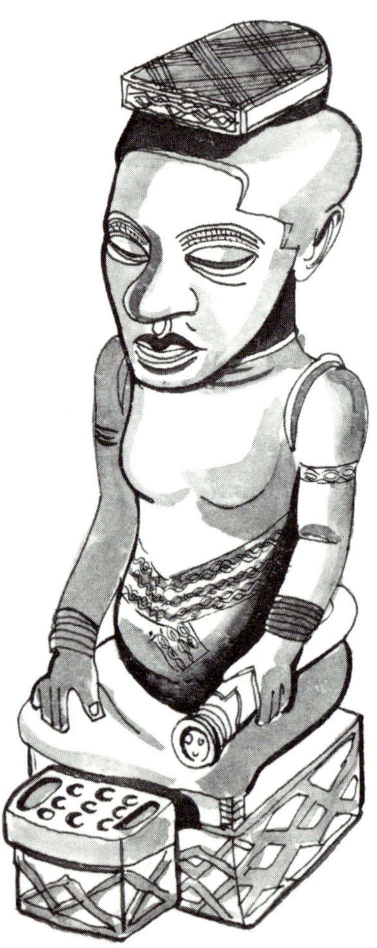

Fig. 18. King Shamba. Wood. Height approximately 6 inches. Zaire. *Circa.* A.D. 1600. Royal portrait of the legendary good king of the Bushongo peoples; famed for his inventions and for discovering new products and abolishing cruel weapons. He sits in front of a Manakala board, a game introduced by him from Arabia to replace gambling.

Colonial Arts

Like fancy titles, labels naming epochs prove frequently misleading. To apply the term "colonial" to the art of Africa during the period of many centuries when the continent was explored, exploited and infiltrated by peoples not native to the soil may be precisely inaccurate. It may serve generally, however, to identify artistic expression produced in Africa under foreign influences, or that which was imported or absorbed by or superimposed upon the indigenous native product described as traditional arts.*

That foreigner marauders deprived, defrauded and destroyed things African, both human and material, cannot be denied. That they also introduced some benefits of Western or Eastern civilization must be granted. That traditional artistic expression in Africa was altered by the contact was inevitable.

Generally speaking, two things happened. One, gradually foreigners destroyed great quantities of African art and carried an incal-

* Foreigners began infiltrating into Nigeria, Zaire and Kenya by at least the eleventh century. The account of these invasions is complex and confusing and beyond the scope of this introductory study.

culable amount of artistic things out of the country; and two, African artistic expression under foreign influence became more secular—less conceptual and functional as magic or religious rite—and more professional and aesthetic.

To explain the first of these generalizations, during these years some zealous missionaries systematically hunted out and destroyed pagan idols. They burned masks and smashed symbolic artifacts they considered abhorrent. In the name of their "more enlightend" religion they may have deprived the world of much of the traditional artistic treasures of Africa. In much the same way bigoted Puritans under Cromwell's "Protectorate" in England lopped off the heads of statues in Canterbury Cathedral. Foreign invaders in Africa may also have carelessly or inadvertently destroyed art objects in the burning and looting they committed to root out and to subdue natives, or perhaps just to "amuse themselves" or to satisfy a whim. Soldiers occupying the refectory of the monastery in Milan are said to have wantonly damaged Da Vinci's painting of the Last Supper by knocking out a portion of the wall to make a more convenient passageway; and during the Egyptian campaign soldiers took pot shots at the age-old face of the sphynx—evidence that there are times when man's inhumanity to man extends to include the things he creates!

Enterprising foreigners during the colonial period in Africa simply lifted enormous quantities of African art—just as Lord Elgin looted the Parthenon in Greece—to take back home for souvenirs or momentoes of "ethnic culture," recognizing their potential value as stock for museum collections. As early as the fifteenth century the Duke of Burgundy had a handsome collection of African sculpture at his estate, and German museums before the sixteenth century, as well as museums in Austria and Sweden, had African artifacts on display.(1)

So foreigners in Africa not only desecrated human beings by selling them into slavery, they also desecrated their artifacts and their religious symbols as well. Some native Africans also—perhaps a considerable number—participated in the vandalism and no doubt profited both from the slave trading and from the selling of merchandise to foreigners. The Europeans, at least, salved their consciences by partial payments to some natives for some of the value received.

Concerning the increase in secularization and the trend toward professionalism, whereas traditionally primitive art was conceptual and functional, being especially concerned with the creation of symbols for use in secret rituals connected with magic or religious rites, during the colonial period craftsmen catered to the interests of foreigners, fashioning masks and figures acceptable to their taste. Gradually some native craftsmen veered toward professionalism in the sense that they made objects for barter or trade. They began to focus upon the aesthetic rather than the ritual. They created objects for public viewing. But, of course, secretly produced artifacts for magic and religious rites continued to be made by the initiates in the areas more or less untouched by foreign influences and no doubt in many infiltrated areas as well. Some of the traditional continued to exist and persist, fortunately, regardless of intervention and innovation. The establishment doesn't get completely unestablished very easily.

KENYA

In west coastal Kenya, Arabs and Persians and Chinese and Indians arrived very early. Ruins of a sultan's palace and a great mosque testify to the infiltration of the Muslims. Barely a hundred years after Columbus discovered America, Portuguese landed there and the remains of Fort Jesus at Monbari built in 1593 still exist. The fort was used by the British later as a jail. Today it houses a museum with still sturdy, sun baked walls facing the sea. Along the Kenyan coast stone statues have been uncovered, the remains of dwellings as well as mosques, and palace ruins—indications of an astonishingly advanced and sophisticated culture brought here from distant lands by peoples not native to Africa. At Gedi, four miles inland, are ruins of a twelfth century city with traces of a great palace compound and a "jami," or chief mosque. (2) The Azanian tribes of coastal east Africa were of mixed blood but predominently Arabian and Portuguese. Theirs was an immigrant culture, primarily Muslim, with mosques dating from the fifteenth century, having elaborate stone stairways and rows of pillars of masonry, tall and tapered in the oriental fashion. (3) They imported from the East iron tools and glass, and silks and brocades from India and China and Arabia. Possibly they never initiated the manufacture of such items, but the imprint of their shapes and their textures and their colors undoubtedly remained in the minds of native Africans.

Along coastal Kenya the Arabs evidently suppressed and destroyed many of the large wooden masks and statues of the Bantus known to have lived in those parts and known to have produced such artifacts elsewhere in the interior of Africa. But the foreigners with their more sophisticated religion did not touch the smaller family crafted symbols used in the celebration of the coming of age and in fertility rites. Or perhaps these could more easily be hidden and thus preserved. Objects of this sort dating from this period still exist along coastal Kenya.

Years later when the British had settled in Kenya they built a railroad clear across the country to Lake Victoria and imported foreign labor from East India and Arabia to do the job. Contemporary statistics indicate that out of approximately eight million inhabitants of Kenya, about a million are foreigners, and of these two hundred thousand are Indians. Besides importing labor, the British obviously also imported both their material necessities and their comforts, their customs and their more than occasional decorative objects for household furnishings, and they built their homes after the fashion of Europe. Many native to Kenya must have observed and imitated, perhaps borrowed, some of these objects.

The Kikuyu tribes of the Bantu groups in Kenya have always been pastoral nomadic peoples who developed little if any very permanent artistic expression, being unsettled and wandering by nature and occupation. Eventually they were virtually destroyed by the great warrior-hunter Masai tribes. And the rebellious Mau Mau insurrection, largely Kikuyu peoples, retaliated—terrorizing both foreign colonials and natives, creating havoc and destruction which has become legendary.

ZAIRE

In the area of central Africa now occupied by the Republic of Zaire, Portuguese missionaries arrived by 1482, making their way down the Congo River into the interior to proselytize the natives and incidentally to suppress their religious practices by destroying their pagan idols. Later the British and the Belgians dominated the country for many years superimposing the influence of their foreign cultures.

Stone statuary dating from the seventeenth century has been discovered in this area of Zaire, statuary so closely resembling that of the Yoruba culture of Nigeria that one might take it as evidence that native African tribal wanderings interpenetrated and brought culture interchange. This may be speculation, however. It is possible that the region's natives developed a similar style independent of the Yoruba. In any event, a high quality of wood carvings with some recognizable regional characteristics—hairdos and facial scarifications faithfully carried out—existed in colonial times. (4)

The Boshongo peoples of central Zaire, like those of Ife and Benin in Nigeria, created portrait carvings of their rulers as memorials and to inspire respect for them. Since they were made of wood, many of these have not survived. The portrait of the famous ninety-third ruler of Boshongo, the great "inventor king," Shamba Bolongongo (*circa* A.D. 1600), however, may be representative [Fig. 18]. Its facial features are probably not realistic but rather idealized representation, just as portraits of the ancient Greek dignitaries depicted spiritual nobility and serenity rather than an actual likeness of their subjects.

The portrait of Shamba depicts the aspects of royalty, an image of the power and divinity of a king, not an individual portrait of any one king. All the trappings of royalty are included: the oddly shaped crown or bonnet, the iron rings around the shoulders, armlets and bracelets, cowrie shells about the abdomen, a short sword in the left hand, and, on the little pedestal jutting out in front, an object associated with the ruler—the game of Mankala which King Shamba is supposed to have introduced to the Congo from Arabia. The serenity of the facial features and the expression of the eyes reveal the calm temper and wisdom of the legendary reputation of a good king.

Here is special evidence of the infiltration of culture in the adaption of the game from Arabia. Indeed King Shamba traditionally was supposed to have been a great traveller who ventured forth to observe and returned with new materials and techniques—the cassava plant from the Portuguese, for instance, and methods of weaving raffia from other tribes in Africa. He is also supposed to have introduced tobacco and the oil palm tree, which bears the name Shamba.

Fetishes and masks employed by the natives for religious and ritual purposes became altered by the addition of European ornamentation—designs, symbols and even facial features not native to Africa. The nail fetish is surely an illustration of the use of foreign materials and objects superimposed upon a basic regional tradition [Fig. 17]. Examples of the nail fetish can be seen in many museums both in Europe and in America. They are usually made of wood, squat and distorted in shape with exaggerated features. Into their bodies have been driven great numbers of iron nails, wedges, or knife blades so that the whole object seems to bristle with jagged barbs. One can only speculate about the significance of the nail fetishes. It may be that, as with the Voodoo dolls of Haiti, the spikes driven into the object were believed to bring pain and discomfort to an enemy. Or it may be that somehow the mysterious protective magic of the fetish was drawn out by the driving in of nails. The whole business is mysterious and irrational; only the initiates knew the secrets of the symbolism—and they never revealed their secrets.

In much the same way the masks of Zaire were ritual objects rather than decorative or aesthetic [Fig. 20-23]. Originally they were rarely viewed by the public, but worn only in secret ceremonies by the initiates and frequently hidden from the spectators by long veils or straw fringes. The spirit behind the mask, perhaps evoked by the drums and the chants, was thought to guide the dancer. Masked dancers at times were kept under control by keepers with ropes to restrain their movements when they became too exuberant. This is like the "principle" of the ouija board in which some "mysterious" power seems to guide the wedge-shaped platform upon which one rests his fingers lightly and makes it move from one to the other of the letters of the alphabet printed on the board, spelling out the answers to questions addressed to it. Or the principle behind the Japanese "mikosi," or portable shrine, carried through the streets on festival days on the shoulders of young men who chant and shout—and apparently the spirit within the shrine causes them to weave from side to side and directs their movements backwards or forwards by the emanation of its power. In like manner the spirit of the mask controlled the dancer, just as the voices of the gods spoke through the drums.

Some of the ancient ceremonies took the form of plays which may have lasted several days. Sometimes the mask of a character or the character itself in one of these ritual performances was borrowed from another village together with the appropriate chants and dance steps. And sometimes the imported mask developed into a new god or spirit for that village, and the artist who fashioned the new mask became a channel of communication with the supernatural. Lineage groups possessed cult objects, masks or statues worn on top of a headdress, which were renewed perhaps every fifty years, the basic forms being handed down from generation to generation of artists. (5) In ancient times any one who saw the mask, even inadvertently, who was not among the initiates, might be put to death.

Today museums display these masks and ritual objects as works of art, as objects for public observation; private collectors display them as decorations upon their walls. This may be a desecration of their original purpose, but the masks of Zaire, both handsome and horrible, do have a peculiar fascination. Some are sad and weary in expression, some horribly distorted with grossly exaggerated features, some seem fairly realistic portraits of specific individuals, some are perky and gleeful. Some of the masks have fiber beards and slanting oriental eyes looking for all the world like some consumptive Chinese patriarch, the nose a geometrically designed elongated triangle.

Surely these masks have aesthetic appeal disassociated from their original religious function. Even the nail fetishes have a peculiar kind of artistic charm. And some of the masks dating from the colonial period, as well as those being fashioned today, show foreign influences, for some of the faces are not indigenous to Africa.

NIGERIA

Nigeria was the epicenter of slave trade during the colonial period. Outsiders came from the Arabian north and the Near East to capture or to barter for slaves; some time later they came from the west and the south—the ubiquitous Portuguese and the British, the Dutch, the French and the Spanish. From northern and interior Nigeria not only were slaves exported but also ivory and gold in return for cloth and salt and coral. Ideas and cultures of the Muslim Arab-Berber peoples, as well as those of the European Christians, infiltrated into Nigeria. The complexity of this interpenetration is impossible to untangle, much less to follow in detail.

Every comprehensive history of Africa refers to the fabulous city of Timbuktu in Mali, northwest of contemporary Nigeria, where a legendary culture existed with a university and famous workshops fashioning iron and leather and where trading caravans with as many as twelve thousand camels visited. But reference is also made to the high degree of culture and commercial development in Bornu in the general area of the Northeastern State of Nigeria. This area was the termination of one of the great caravan routes from Cairo. To the west of Bornu were seven Hausa states grouped together as a protective military unit. Here they grew cotton and made cloth and objects of iron.

Kano in the north central region of Nigeria produced dyed cloth —characteristically deep blue in color—and leather goods, and exported ostrich feathers and slaves. (6) People of the Kano region fashioned clay pots and vessels decorated with pictures of snakes and birds and geometric designs; they devised ornate calabashes (hollowed out gourds) and used beads and cowrie shells to ornament cloth for headdresses and garments. Kano is a region of horn-blowers, famous for their seven-foot-long trumpets fashioned by the Hausa tribes. And natives from this region built boxlike houses with mud walls dyed pink [Fig. 19]. In the area are ruins of mosques with towering minarets as evidence of Muslim cultural influence.

In the south of Nigeria the Yoruba kingdoms with descendants from two main groups—the indigenous stock for whom Ife was a sacred place and the invading peoples from the north—had by the sixteenth century a well-organized society with considerable trade, primarily in salt. When a Portuguese adventurer, the first recorded European visitor, arrived in 1486, the Benin culture was well established and of sufficient interest to attract merchants. The English arrived as early as 1553. According to Michael Crowder in *The Story of Nigeria,* quoted by an official publication of the Nigerian Embassy, the Europeans found a kingdom "highly organized, backed by a large and efficient army, which gave it control of a large area of the coast . . . its economy was such as to allow not only for sacred carvings . . . but for a great deal of secular art, such as superbly carved ornaments, bells, lamp holders, doors and pillars, many of which are now scattered throughout the museums of the world." (7)

Examples of Benin arts and crafts were excavated in 1934 by Mr. Kenneth C. Murray, the British archaeologist and antiquarian, in the ruins of the palaces of the obas, but large portions of ancient Benin art, including bronze heads and sacred ivories, had already been removed to the British Museum and to museums in Germany. (8)

It is not the purpose here to attempt to untangle the complicated skein of African history. But the Benin culture of Yorubaland (Nigeria) in most accounts seems roughly to correspond to the late Middle Ages and the Renaissance of European cultures. During this period many confusing tribal conflicts occurred. At neighboring Ife the "Oni," or Divine Ruler, was considered a descendent of Odudua, one of the three Gods sent down from heaven by Olorun to create the earth which was scratched up out of the sea at Ife. The Oni of Ife might be compared with the Pope of Christendom residing in Rome. From the Oni were delegated the various Oba of Benin who received their power to rule from this divinely instituted authority. The analogy with the Pope is inexact, but the comparison might help one to understand the somewhat peculiar circumstances and the inter-involvement of Benin with Ife. The Benin Oba, according to some accounts, was confined to the palace enclosure and supervised by the priests, but he was attended upon with magnificent ceremony and a great display of wealth. There are repeated references to "bloody Benin" because of the prevalence of human sacrifice.

Sometime after the establishment of the Oba dynasties, skilled craftsmen were sent for from Ife to establish foundries in Benin territories and to teach Benin craftsmen the necessary techniques to make bronze portraits locally as a record of historical events or royal personages. Although some of the Benin sculptured bronzes may be somewhat inferior to those of Ife, they are handsome, considerably varied in style, artistically decorative and marvelously clear as records of costumes and customs. [Fig. 12-16]. Some of the Benin bronzes are of Europeans, most particularly the Portuguese; many of them show ornamentation of foreign design.

A very famous Benin bronze is the portrait of the Queen Mother [Fig. 14]—a beautifully serene face, obviously regal, surmounted by a tall peaked cap or headdress with a curiously horn-like twist, and decorated with cross-hatching. Others portray the stalwart Obas themselves, their faces partially stylized under a kind of basketweave cap and buried neck and chin in a heavy collar of coral [Fig. 13]. Some of these Oba heads support an entire tusk of ivory on top. One portrait shows the fourteenth century Oba with the legs of a mudfish supported by an attendant on each side. The figures have helmet-like headdresses with sharply pointed tops; they appear to be wearing long-sleeved, knee-length coats of mail. Two of the bronze figures are very short and squat, possibly pygmy slaves or maybe midgets employed as court jesters [Fig. 15]. One is the figure of a musician in a skirt playing a flute. There are figures on horseback carrying weapons; several wear what appear to be Christian crosses about the neck. One figure depicts a Portuguese aiming a crossbow. And there are many bronze plaques showing scenes at court, ceremonials, and various customs.

Armlets and small masks fashioned from ivory also date from this period, as well as ivory gongs and elaborately carved heads of staffs or scepters.

As living symbols of power and authority, leopards had been used as palace guardians for the Obas of Benin; apparently they were also household pets. Benin craftsmen fashioned handsome bronze figures of leopards complete with stylized spots [Fig. 12]. Some of the animal figures are hollow and have moveable jaws; they were used as containers for water. All of them are decorative and attractive and surprisingly modern in design. Surprisingly modern also are the bronzed figures of birds, probably cocks.

In southern Nigeria, ruins of an ancient palace compound of a Benin tribe include remains of wooden pillars in a colonade structure; the pillars are covered entirely with a coating or veneer of bronze. Etched into the bronze are scenes from the hunt, or battles, or portraits of royal personages. Over two thousand etched pictures are preserved in a recognizable condition because metal, of course, lasts longer than wood and resists decay and destruction by the elements or by man.

The Benin Obas grew materially rich as the economy of the Benin Empire expanded. There is a legend about an emissary sent to Europe as representative of the Oba of Benin laden with fabulous gifts of ivory and gold, with multitudes of attendants splendidly garbed, rather like oriental potentates. And the legend persists that among other gifts and artifacts brought along by the Oba's representatives was the spoon —thus introducing to European civilization this implement of etiquette previously unknown there.

Not only did the envoys from the Obas of Benin bring splendid gifts from Africa to Portugal; they also brought back to Africa European wares, woven cloth, ornaments and utensils. The designs of these things must have influenced African artisans. Also, Yoruba slaves returning as freedmen from Brazil and elsewhere (a considerable number did succeed in escaping bondage in one way or another) brought back with them ideas for shapes and styles which may quite conceivably have influenced building and crafts. Music and dancing were similarly influenced.

Famous Nigerian bronze statues were discovered along the middle Niger at Jebba and Tada; these were said to have been brought from elsewhere as symbols of prestige. Those found at Jebba are of military bowmen, larger and heavier in design than the Benin bronzes, ornamented, and austere in expression. One of the seven portraits found at Jeda has caused much favorable comment in museum exhibitions to which it has been loaned by the Nigerian government [Fig. 1]. It is a statue of a figure seated with one knee upright. Although both hands and portions of one leg are missing, probably due to constant ritual rubbing with sand and water, enough of the statue remains to reveal the serenity of the rather Buddha-like pose and the calm face.

DANCING

Writing his observations as a missionary during the period of foreign infiltration, G. T. Basden includes in his book *Among the Ibos of Nigeria* this account of the dancing:

Dancing is the great national pastime, and it is practiced by everybody capable of movement. There are many forms—for boys, for girls, for men, for women and for mixed companies, the last being more especially associated with religious observances and festivals. It is the religious element which distinguishes the set forms of dancing from those which are the outcome of the emotions.

The stereotyped set dances are all performed by professional men, and they are very elaborate and extraordinarily difficult and exhausting. The movements are perfectly rhythmic, and the time is set by music. The instruments are crude but effective. One youth grips in each hand a carafe-shaped calabash (awyaw) surrounded by flounces of cowrie shells, and these are rattled with methodical vigour, producing a sound not unlike the backwash of waves on a shingly beach. Another youth hugs closely under his left arm a clay pot from ten to twelve inches in diameter. It has two holes, one at the top of the neck, the other in the side. To make music the performer beats sharply upon the mouth with the open palm of his right hand, the left hand, meanwhile, being passed backwards and forwards over the side-hole. The effect is not unpleasant; it is a sort of mellow booming sound which rises and falls as the side-hole is covered or left open. There may be wind instruments also, short reeds pierced with three holes for fingering; these give highly pitched notes more like those of a piccolo. In addition there are drums—small and great—which are also capable of variation in note by pressure of the left hand over different parts of the surface.

The instrumentalists squat on the ground in no prescribed order, with neither programme nor conductor. Presently one of the musicians sounds a few desultory notes, which gradually evolve into a recognised melody, the others join in, and time and tune are thus established. The dancers range themselves and begin slow rhythmic movements, unconsciously swaying their heads in time with the music. As the dance proceeds they appear intoxicated with the motion and the music, the speed increases, and the movements become more and more intricate and bewildering. The dancers work themselves into a veritably frenzy and the spectators keep silence from sheer excitement. The twistings, turnings, contortions and springing movements, executed in perfect time, are wonderful to behold. Movement succeeds movement in rapid succession, speed and force increasing, until the grand finale is reached. By this time the onlookers, as well as the dancers, are almost breathless. Then, in a flash, music and dance cease abruptly, the performers remaining rigid in their last pose. For a second absolute silence prevails, followed by an outburst of applause. The effect of the sudden arrest of music and motion cannot be described; it breaks upon one with such an unexpected shock. The dancers are streaming with perspiration and quite exhausted with their efforts. The sign for the dance to end is given by the chief drummer, the dancers themselves, naturally, having a pretty clear idea when to expect it. For these set dances, e.g. those executed by the "Guinea-fowl dancers," the physical strength required is tremendous. The body movements are extremely difficult and would probably kill a European. The whole anatomy of the performer appears to be in serious danger, and it is a marvel that his internal machinery is not completely thrown out of gear. The practice of such dancing leads to a wonderful development of the back and abdominal muscles. Moreover the movements are free, there is nothing rigid about them, and they produce no sign of "physical exerciser" stiffness. Every movement is clean, sure and decided, showing absolute control of the muscles. For some of the dances the performers wear clusters of shells around one or both ankles, and these are shaken simultaneously by all the members of the party. The precision with which this is done, and the execution of the many intricate figures, are marvelous.

The professional dancers are very well paid for their services, and when fulfilling an engagement are liberally entertained. The dances are not all uniform; usually the displays of one town differ in character and movement from those of its neighbours.

Of quite another type is the dancing connected with religious festivities, and particularly that in which women take a leading part. Such dancing is always the physical expression of joy and thanksgiving. It consists almost entirely of strange sinuous movements of the limbs and body. If these movements are the expressions of the primeval idea of dancing, then, to judge by the illustrated papers, a great deal of so-called dancing in England and America is merely a reversion to type. It would appear that the exponents of twentieth century dancing are engaged in a feeble imitation of the first.

In all native dances each man (and woman) acts independently of his fellows and yet fits into his proper place in the general scheme. When men and women are dancing in company they do not even touch hands. It is contrary to etiquette for a man to touch a woman, and any infringement of the rule may meet with stern rebuke. As a matter of fact each person becomes so completely absorbed in the dance that any interference would give rise to emphatic protest and annoyance. I have watched such dances and can testify to the extraordinary manner in which the dancers, for the time being, lose consciousness of their surroundings. One stands before them, and they give no sign of recognition; one speaks, but there is no response other than a fixed stare. Only gradually do they become normal again.

The dances are always held in the open air, but not always in a public place. Frequently they are held in the compound of a chief or other prominent man. In either case it is a hot and dusty pastime, and hence is invariably associated with heavy drinking. After joining in a few short figures at the beginning of the festival many of the old men find it difficult to rise from their seats of honour with any degree of steadiness.

Some of the movements are peculiar, as when the lower limbs are kept perfectly rigid the feet are not lifted from the ground, but all progression is made by swaying the body only, and by sinuous movements.

The pastime has a fascination of its own, and even the spectator finds it difficult to keep his feet and body from moving in sympathy with the dancers. As one watches the swaying figures, and listens to the rhythm of the music, one naturally responds. It is doubtful whether any native could resist the spell inwardly, whatever outward aspect he might assume—and this is no matter for surprise to those who have been present at such a dance. (9)

Summary

In Africa interchange of culture from outside the continent came very early and continues to the present day. The work of Klee and Picasso notably show influence of African traditional style. Reciprocally the work of black African natives like Yemi Bisiri and Ovia Idah and Lamidi Fakeye, to mention only three, reveal the mixture of the western culture with the traditional African culture. Some African artists were taught European methods; others observed and absorbed, unconsciously adapting.

That the culture and the indigenous artistic expression of African peoples were greatly influenced by this influx of foreigners is abundantly evident. Yet indigenous culture and traditional native expression, both religious and secular, in so complex and vast a country persisted—never becoming completely absorbed by foreign influences.

Colonial African Writing

These selections reflect foreign influences on native African writers and their comments concerning Africa under foreign control or supervision. Relatively little seems to have been written by native Africans during this period—quite probably because foreigners who dominated the country were rarely interested in encouraging native writing; also because literacy was not high and until recently very few of the spoken languages were written languages. African literature in the oral tradition, naturally, continued during this period and much of this was revised and adjusted to fit the new conditions.

Local Customs and Early Life

O. EQUIANO

From *The Interesting Narrative of the Life of Olaudah Equiano or Gustavus Vassa the African,* 3rd ed. (enlarged), London, 1790.

O. Equiano was born in 1745(6) at Essaka, some distance from Benin, and carried off into slavery during his early teens. After service as a slave in America he was freed, and after travelling extensively on merchant ships he settled in England.

We compute the year from the day on which the sun crosses the line, and on its setting that evening, there is a general shout throughout the land; at least I can speak from my own knowledge, throughout our vicinity. The people at the same time make a great noise with rattles, not unlike the basket rattles used by children here, though much larger, and hold up their hands to heaven for a blessing. It is then the greatest offerings are made, and those children whom our wise men foretell will be fortunate are then presented to different people. I remember many used to come to see me, and I was carried about for that purpose. They have many offerings, particularly at full moons; generally two at harvest before the fruits are taken out of the ground: and when any young animals are killed, sometimes they offer up part of them as a sacrifice. These offerings, when made by one of the heads of a family, serve for the whole. I remember we often had them at my father's and my uncle's, and their families have been present. Some of our offerings are eaten with bitter herbs. We had a saying among us to anyone of a cross temper, 'That if they were to be eaten, they should be eaten with bitter herbs.'

We practised circumcision like the Jews, and made offerings and feasts on that occasion in the same manner as they did. Like them, also, our children were named from some event, some circumstance, or fancied foreboding at the time of their birth. I was named *Olaudah*, which, in our language, signifies 'vicissitude', or fortunate also; one favoured, and having a loud voice and well spoken. I remember we never polluted the name of the object of our adoration; on the contrary, it was always mentioned with the greatest reverence; and we were totally unacquainted with swearing, and all those terms of abuse and reproach which find their way so readily and copiously into the language of more civilized people. The only expressions of that kind I remember were, 'May you rot, or may you swell, or may a beast take you.'

I have before remarked that the natives of this part of Africa are extremely clean. This necessary habit of decency was with us a part of religion, and therefore we had many purifications and washings; indeed almost as many, and used on the same occasions, if my recollection does not fail me, as the Jews. Those that touched the dead at any time were obliged to wash and purify themselves before they could enter a dwelling-house. Every woman too, at certain times, was forbidden to come into a dwelling-house, or touch any person or any thing we eat. I was so fond of my mother I could not keep from her, or avoid touching her at some of those periods, in consequence of which I was obliged to be kept out with her, in a little house made for that purpose, till offering was made, and then we were purified.

Though we had no places of public worship, we had priests and magicians, or wise men. I do not remember whether they had different offices, or whether they were united in the same persons, but they were held in great reverence by the people. They calculated our time, and foretold events, as their name imported, for we called them Ah-affoc-way-cah, which signifies 'calculators' or 'yearly men', our year being called Ah-affoc. They wore their beards, and when they died they were succeeded by their sons. Most of their implements and things of value were interred along with them. Pipes and tobacco were also put into the grave with the corpse, which was always perfumed and ornamented, and animals were offered in sacrifice to them. None accompanied their funerals but those of the same profession or tribe. These buried them after sunset, and always returned from the grave by a different way from that which they went.

These magicians were also our doctors or physicians. They practised bleeding by cupping; and were very successful in healing wounds and expelling poison. They had likewise some extraordinary method of discovering jealousy, theft, and poisoning; the success of which no doubt they derived from the unbounded influence over the credulity and superstition of the peoples. I do not remember what those methods were, except that as to poisoning: I recollect an instance or two, which I hope it will not be deemed impertinent here to insert, as it may serve as a kind of specimen of the rest, and is still used by the Negroes in the West Indies. A young woman had been poisoned, but it was not known by whom: the doctors ordered the corpse to be taken up by some persons, and carried to the grave. As soon as the bearers had raised it on their shoulders, they seemed seized with some sudden impulse and ran to and fro unable to stop themselves. At last, after having passed through a number of thorns and prickly bushes unhurt, the corpse fell from them close to a house, and defaced it in the fall; and the owner being taken up, he immediately confessed the poisoning. . . . I have already acquainted the reader with the time and place of my birth. My father, besides many slaves, had a numerous family, of which seven lived to grow up, including myself and a sister, who was the only daughter. As I was the youngest of the sons, I became, of course, the greatest favourite with my mother, and was always with her; and she used to take particular pains to form my mind. I was trained up from my earliest years in the art of war: my daily exercise was shooting and throwing javelins; and my mother adorned me with emblems, after the manner of our greatest warriors. In this way I grew up till I was turned the age of eleven, when an end was put to my happiness in the following manner:—

Generally when the grown people in the neighbourhood were gone far in the fields to labour, the children assembled together in some of the neighbour's premises to play; and commonly some of us used to get up a tree to look out for any assailant, or kidnapper, that might come upon us; for they sometimes took those opportunities of our parents' absence, to attack and carry off as many as they could seize. One day as I was watching at the top of a tree in our yard. I saw one of those people come into the yard of our next neighbour but one, to kidnap, there being many stout young people in it. Immediately on this I gave the alarm of the rogue, and he was surrounded by the stoutest of them, who entangled him with cords, so that he could not escape till some of the grown people came and secured him. But alas! ere long it was my fate to be thus attacked and to be carried off, when none of the grown people were nigh. One day, when all our people were gone out to their work as usual, and only I and my dear sister were left to mind the house, two men and a woman got over our walls, and in a moment seized us both; and, without giving us time to cry out, or make resistance, they stopped our mouths, and ran off with us into the nearest wood. Here they tied our hands, and continued to carry us as far as they could, till night came on, when we reached a small house, where the robbers halted for refreshment and spent the night. We were then unbound, but were unable to take any food; and being quite over-powered by fatigue and grief, our only relief was some sleep, which allayed our misfortune for a short time. The next morning we left the house, and continued travelling all the day. For a long time we had kept the woods, but at last we came into a road which I believed I knew. I now had some hopes of being delivered; for we had advanced but a little way before I discovered some people at a distance, on which I began to cry out for their assistance; but my cries had no other effect than to make them tie me faster and stop my mouth, and then they put me into a large sack. They also stopped my sister's mouth, and tied her hands; and in this manner we proceeded till we were out of the sight of these people. When we went to rest the following night they offered us some victuals; but we refused it; and the only comfort we had was in being in one another's arms all that night, and bathing each other with our tears. But alas! we were soon deprived of even the small comfort of weeping together. The next day proved of greater sorrow than I had yet experienced; for my sister and I were then separated, while we lay clasped in each other's arms: it was in vain that we besought them not to part us; she was torn from me, and immediately carried away, while I was left in a state of distraction not to be described. I cried and grieved continually; and for several days did not eat any thing but what they forced into my mouth. At length, after many days travelling, during which I had often changed masters, I got into the hands of a chieftain, in a very pleasant country. This man had two wives and some children, and they all used me extremely well, and did all they could to comfort me; particularly the first wife, who was something like my mother. Although I was a great many days journey from my father's house, yet these people spoke exactly the same language with us. This first master of mine, as I may call him, was a smith, and my principal employment was working his bellows, which were the same kind I had seen in my vicinity. They were in some respects not unlike the stoves here in gentlemen's kitchens; and were covered with leather; and in the middle of that leather a stick was fixed, and a person stood up, and worked it, in the same manner as is done to pump water out of a cask with a hand pump. I believe it was gold he worked, for it was of a lovely bright yellow colour, and was worn by the women on their wrists and ankles. I was there I suppose about a month and they at last used to trust me some little distance from the house.

(Nigeria)

The Death of Captain Moloney

I was born in my father's house near the Kofar Kokona in Keffi. My father was Tumbudi the barber. When I was a youth of twenty my father died and, thrown upon my own resources, I entered the household of Dan Ya Musa, the Magaji of Keffi, as a retainer. I got this place because I was a friend of Ladan, a son of the Magaji, who spoke to his father on my behalf. I was in the Magaji's household for two years before Captain Moloney, whom we called 'Mai Launi', arrived in Keffi just before the rains.

The Magaji, Dan Ya Musa, was a very short man indeed, not more than five feet two inches at the most. Although short, he was of well-proportioned build, neither fat nor slim. He always wore a black beard, but no side whiskers. His teeth in particular were small and well formed and he had not lost any.

He was dark skinned for a Fulani, and he was a fine horseman, hunter, and warrior. When opposed he was of an extremely fiery temper and could then be severe.

He was full of zest and vigour and had four wives and many concubines. Without doubt he was the most powerful man in Keffi, even more powerful than the Emir.

Although I did not know his age, I knew that he was in the prime of life.

His role in Keffi was that of a supervisor on behalf of the Emir of Zaria, whose fief Keffi was.

His hobby was war. Each dry season he used to go out against the Toni pagans of Dari, Amba, and Riri and the Mada pagans south-east of his headquarters which he built at Kokona. . . .

To Dan Ya Musa slaves were money. Cola-nuts, gowns, trousers were all paid for in slaves and every year a tribute was sent to Zaria and the Sultan. Every year also a large number of horses used to come down from the north for the Magaji's men to ride on and slaves were given in exchange for them.

The first news that we in Keffi had of the doings of the Europeans was brought by a group of Tijani who had been driven out of their country by the French. They passed on to Bauchi. Then later men from Bida came to tell us of the war waged there by the men of the Company.

After I had been with the Magaji two years, Moloney came. When he came the Magaji was sent for and told that there was to be no war and all slaving was to cease. Moloney said 'If the pagans trouble you, tell me and I will deal with them, but you may not.'

The Magaji was most upset at this as slaving was his livelihood, and now it was gone.

However, accompanying Moloney was a man whose name was Webster, whom we called Mallam Bature.

About two months after Moloney arrived a lot of soldiers came to

Keffi and he set off with them to make war on Abuja. They were successful for they sacked the town, captured the Chief, and caught the brigands who were holding the road to ransom.

Moloney was wounded in the leg in this campaign and was carried about in a hammock thereafter.

Webster had been left behind at Keffi and during this time he managed to get on terms of the greatest friendship with the Magaji. He was a constant visitor to Kokona and was always a most welcome guest. I knew him well and liked him, and we all regarded him as our protector.

Moloney's chief Government Agent, on the other hand, was Audu Timtim. He was a liar and a rogue and was utterly without scruples. He set himself to play Moloney off against the Magaji and vice versa. He lied to both about what the other said, and the Magaji was put in great fear of Moloney.

The war with Abuja did not last two months and Moloney and some of the soldiers returned to Keffi. The others went back to Lokoja. Relations between the Magaji and Moloney went from bad to worse, but Webster was always an honoured friend.

One Wednesday the Magaji went into Keffi as usual and on the following day received a summons from Moloney. He sent back a message saying that he had scabies and was treating it and could not go. He did in fact have scabies on his thigh and was bathing the place.

Early on the morning of the Friday (3 October 1902)Moloney arose and left his rest-house in the town. He took his soldiers with him as an escort but left some at his quarters on guard. He was carried in his hammock down to the Emir's palace. With him went Audu Timtim and his second messenger, a man called Musan Gana.

They went into the Emir's palace. I was watching from the Magaji's compound which is only a short distance away. In front of the Emir's palace was a square. On one side was the Emir's house and on the other the Magaji's. After a while the Emir and Moloney came out of the palace. Moloney had dismounted from the hammock and limped out with the Emir. A chair was placed for Moloney and the Emir sat on a mat; a lot of people gathered round.

The soldiers were on one side of the square as well, near the Emir's gateway. Webster was with Moloncy.

After Moloney and the Emir had seated themselves a messenger was sent to summon the Magaji to the square. He refused to come.

Webster then made two journeys to his friend the Magaji to try and persuade him, but it was no good.

Time passed by; eleven o'clock came, and then nearly noon and still the Magaji refused to come. The Emir again sent saying 'Those who are with me are tiring of this game of waiting.' Still the Magaji refused to come.

I heard later that Moloney said he wished to come himself and get him, but the Emir prevented this.

Again Webster was sent and this time the Magaji agreed, and said: 'Wait a little longer, I am coming.' Webster came out of the Magaji's house and walked away across the square. I did not notice where he went, whether to Moloney or the soldiers.

Eventually, the Magaji appeared, riding through the archway of his house. He was mounted on his war-horse, a stallion called 'Dan Ashalu' and he was accompanied by both mounted men and footmen of his bodyguard. I was with the rest of the footmen watching from the entrance to his house.

I saw him ride across the square and approach the Emir as if to give him the traditional salute with his spears. Then I heard a shot. I did not know at the time who fired or at what.

The Magaji always went about armed with two pistols, one of which contained six bullets. He would never be parted from them. One was hidden under his left armpit under his gown and the other was kept in a pouch on his right hip, also concealed by his gown.

When he was shot Moloney fell from his chair. The crowd in the square began to scream and the soldiers started firing. Webster took refuge in the Mosque. Audu Timtim ran away from the square in the direction of the quarter guard at Moloney's house. The Magaji shouted 'Do not touch Mallam Bature.'

At this same time some one in the Magaji's retinue fired an arrow which hit the Emir in the right foot. Pandemonium reigned. The soldiers were firing at the Magaji trying to shoot him. It was a pure miracle that they did not. Bullets were falling in the crowd and there were many killed and wounded.

The Magaji turned his horse and galloped off after Audu Timtim. In the Ungwan Alkali there stood a baobab tree. As Audu Timtim reached this tree the Magaji overtook him and, wheeling his horse, slashed him across the belly with the knife edge of his fighting stirrups and ripped his bowels out. This was only a few score yards away from where I was. Then Barga, a slave of Adamu Maidoka, cut off Audu Timtim's head. Another man cut off Moloney's head and it was thrown down a well outside the gate of the mosque. By the time I returned to Keffi this well had been sealed up on the orders of the Emir.

The troops, who had still been firing, now set off after the Magaji. The horsemen were galloping out of the town and we for our part fled as quickly as we could to Kokona.

The Magaji rode first to Keffin Shanu, about ten miles, and cut the telegraph wire with his sword.

Then Dan Ya Musa turned north and rode beyond Kokona and again cut the wire. This was the wire to Laffia. At the same time he called in his cattle from Keffin Shanu and from Hadari. Then the Magaji returned to Kokona, where we were awaiting him.

He summoned us all together and said 'Today I have dug my own grave. If you wish, leave me and go or if you wish, stay.'

Many of us stayed for the trust we had in him and we were three days in Keffi before a messenger from the Emir came. The Emir sent him to say that there were in Keffi many women and children, many aged, sick, blind, and infirm. If the Magaji remained, all these would be slaughtered when the town was sacked by the soldiers, as sacked it would be. The Emir wished him to be gone. If not, their blood would be on his head.

Next morning the Magaji had his gun fired as was his habit when he wished us to be up and doing. Again he summoned the people saying: 'Those who wish to stay, stay, and those who wish to come with me, come, for I am away to Kano since there are Europeans at Zaria.' We assembled to go with him, well over a hundred fighting men.

Then the Magaji gathered his women and his horses and his cattle. There were about forty women, some seventy horses, and six herds of cattle. We set out from Kokona driving these before us. There were with us some Kano men who acted as guides.

First we went to Akwanga, then . . . to Kachiya. Here we met with some hunters who led us through the bush, which they knew well, so that we might avoid Zaria where the Europeans were . . . And so in twenty-five days we came to Kano.

The Emir sent his men to meet us on the road, and to lead us into the city. Once in the city we were made much of and honoured. We were given houses and cattle and rams and food. There were perhaps fifty of us left of those who had set out from Keffi.

Source: Concerning Brave Captains by D. J. M. Muffett, London, 1964. The narrator is a Hausa called Hassan Keffi.

The background to this story is that Keffi, a satellite of Zaria, was part of the Fulani Empire of Sokoto. When the British proclaimed the Protectorate of Northern Nigeria, however, Keffi was also included in the Province of Nassarawa. It thus became a bone of contention between the two powers whose relations with one another were still governed by vague treaties which evaded all the difficult issues. As a result, the capital of this little Emirate contained two Residents, one Fulani and the other British, and a clash between them became increasingly probable.

The killing of Moloney which is described here assumed considerable historical importance because it finally convinced Lugard, the British High Commissioner, that he had to force a showdown with the Sultan of Sokoto and of course it provided him with a good reason for doing so. It therefore became the *casus belli* which led to the campaign of 1903 and the final downfall of the Fulani Empire.

(Hausa, Nigeria)

The Legend of Daura

There was once a prince of Bagdad called Abuyazidu who quarrelled with his father and left his home in the east. After some time his wanderings brought him to Bornu. There he was given a daughter of the Sultan in marriage, Magira by name. He stayed in Bornu and his affairs prospered so much that in the course of time he became rich and powerful. His wealth and authority only excited hatred and envy, however, and the Sultan began to plot against his life. But Magira, being a daughter of the palace, heard what was afoot and warned her husband. Although she was with child, they decided that the only safety lay in flight. So with nothing but a mule to carry their possessions and a slave-girl to wait on them, they took the road to the west. When they reached a place called Garun Gabas Magira's days were fulfilled and she gave birth to a son. Abuyazidu left her there and, taking the concubine with him, continued his journey.

After a time Abuyazidu came to the town of Daura which was then ruled by a woman, the last of a line of nine Queens. He lodged in the house of an old woman called Waira and in the evening he asked her for water. 'Young man' said the old woman 'in this town there is no water to be had except on Fridays. Only when all the people are assembled can we draw water.'

'Nevertheless' he said 'I am going to get some now. Give me a bucket.'

He took the bucket which she gave him and went to the well. Now a gigantic snake called 'Sarki' lived in the well and when it heard the bucket being lowered it lifted its head out of the well and tried to strike Abuyazidu. But he drew his sword and struck off his head which he then hid. After that he drew water for himself and his horse, gave what was left to the old woman, and went to bed.

Next day as soon as it was light the townspeople saw that the snake was dead. They marvelled at its size and the news was quickly taken to the Queen. Escorted by all her warriors, she rode down to the place and she too marvelled at the size of the snake which was still lying half in and half out of the well. 'I swear' she said 'that if I find the man who killed this snake I will divide the town into two and give half of it to him.'

'It was I' said one of the bystanders at once.

'Where is its head then?' said the Queen. 'If you cannot produce the head you are lying.' The man remained silent. Others also came forward and said that they had killed the snake but none of them could produce the head and their claims were all rejected.

At length the old woman Waira spoke up. 'Yesterday evening' she said 'a stranger came and lodged at my house with a strange animal as big as an ox. He took my bucket, went to the well, drew water, drank some himself, watered his animal, and gave the rest to me. Perhaps it was he who killed the snake.'

'Let him be found' said the Queen. When Abuyazidu appeared she asked him if he had killed the snake. He said that he had and when she demanded its head he produced it from where it was hidden. 'I made a promise' she said 'that I would divide my town in two and give half to him who did this deed.'

'Do not divide the town' he said 'because I for my part will be amply rewarded if you will deign to take me as your consort.' And so it came about that Abuyazidu, Prince of Bagdad, married the Queen of Daura.

After the marriage Abuyazidu took up his residence in the palace. He was given the title of Makas-Sarki, the slayer of the snake, but after a time he came to be known simply as Sarki.

The concubine who had come from Bornu with Abuyazidu now gave birth to a boy. As the Queen seemed to be barren, the girl was confident that one day her son would become Chief so she called him Karabgari or Take-the-Town. But a year or two later the Queen also conceived and in due course she too brought forth a boy. Her son she named Bawogari or Give-back-the-Town.

In the fulness of time Makas-Sarki and the Queen died and they were succeeded by their son. Bawogari thus became the first Chief of Daura and he in turn had six sons. The eldest Gazaura succeeded him in Daura. The second, by the same mother, was Bagaudu and he became the founder of Kano. The third was Gunguma and he became the founder of Zazzau. The fourth was Duma and he became the founder of Gobir. The fifth was Kumayau and he became the founder of Katsina. The youngest was Zuma Kogi and he became the founder of Rano.

Daura, Kano, Zazzau, Gobir, Katsina, and Rano are six of the seven original Hausa States. The seventh is Garun Gabas and that was founded by the son of Abuyzidu's first wife Magira, the daughter of the Sultan of Bornu, whom he had to leave behind when he was on his way from Bornu to Daura.

These are the origins of the *Hausa Bakwai* or seven original states of Hausaland.

(Hausa, Nigeria)

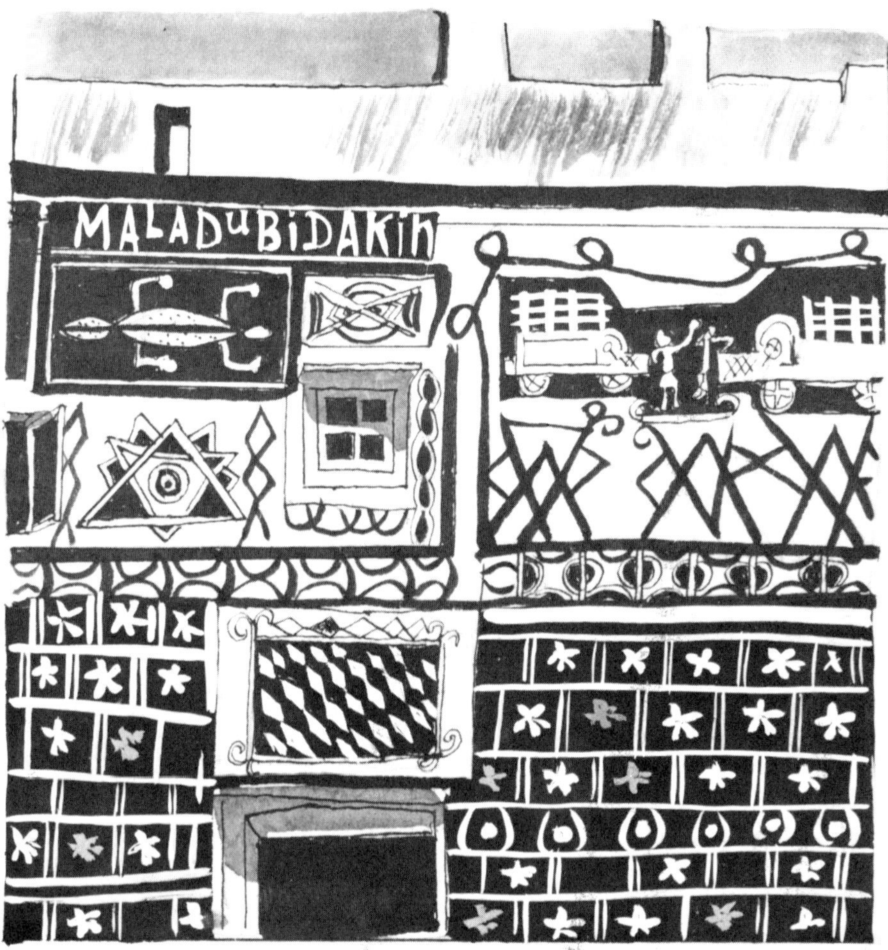

Fig. 19. House decoration, exterior. Paint on plaster; covers the entire house. Hausa, Nigeria. Elaborate designs like this, in vivid color, frequently decorate houses in northern Nigeria; the Mbari house designs are similar.

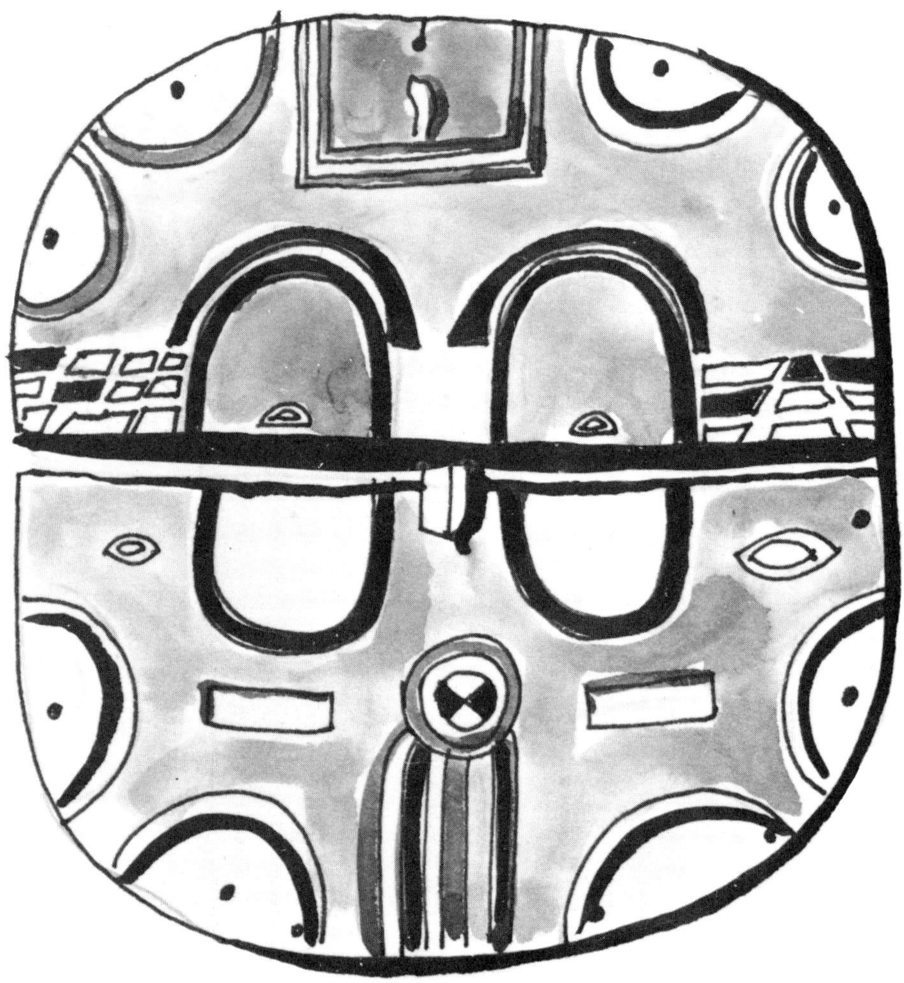

Fig. 20. Bateke Mask. Wood and paint. Life-size. Zaire. An example of almost complete abstraction. Designs like this may have influenced the work of Picasso.

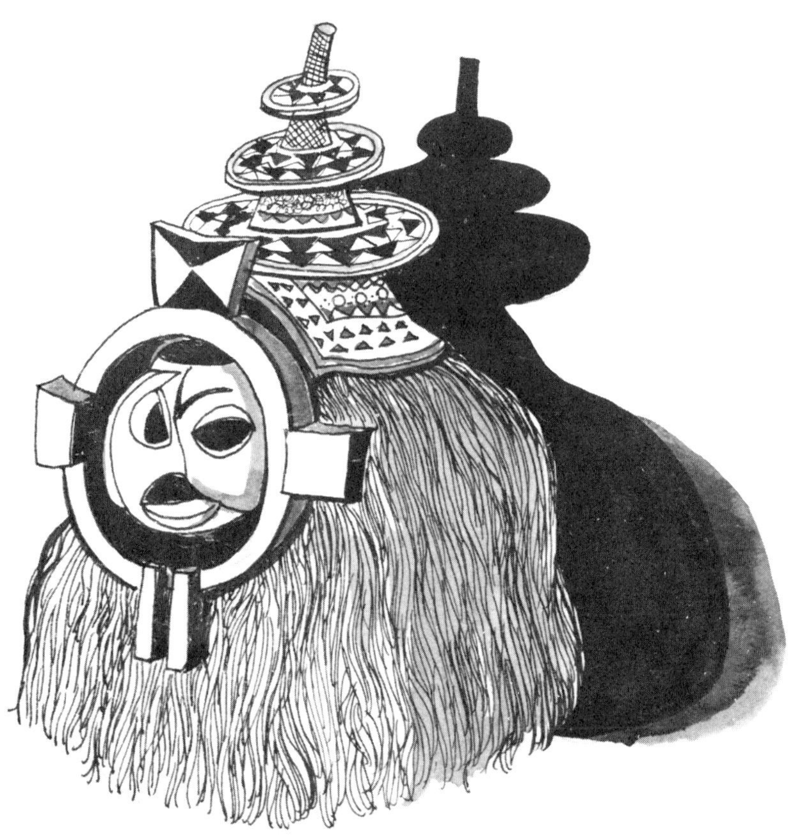

Fig. 21. Bayaka Mask. Wood, paint, raffia. Height approximately 21 inches. Zaire. Work of a southern Bantu tribe. The mask and headdress, with raffia drapery hanging down over the shoulders, completely disguises the performer.

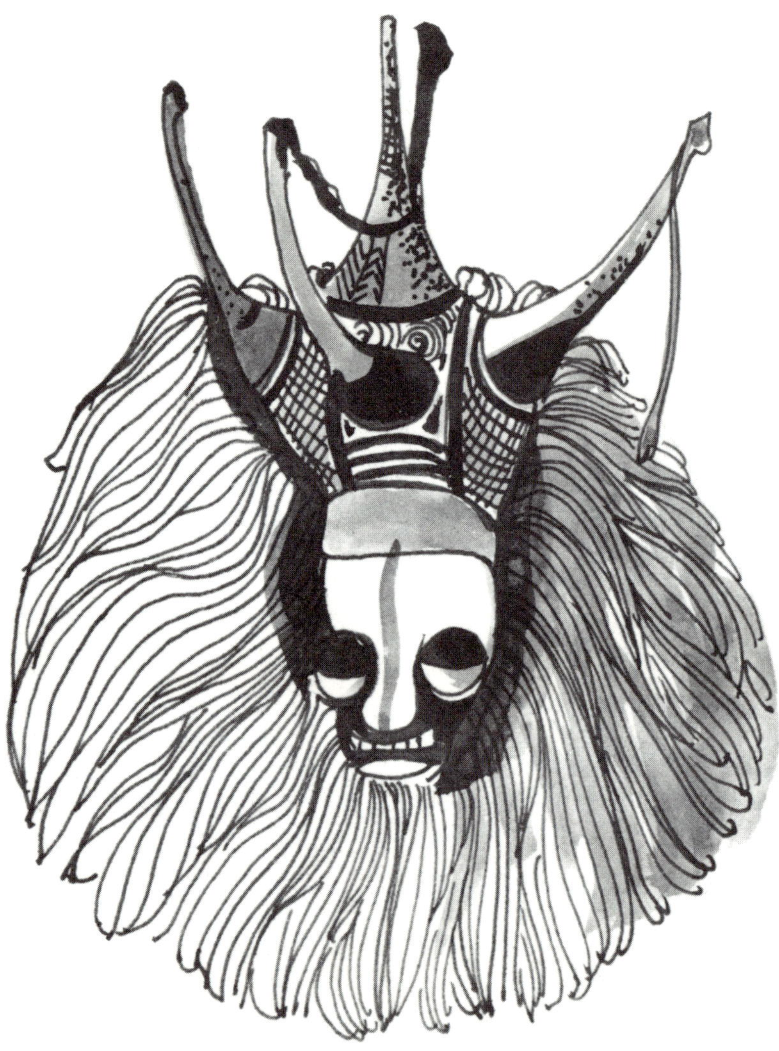

Fig. 22. Bayaka Mask. Wood, paint, antelope horns, raffia. Height 25 inches. Zaire. Worn with raffia capes, the disguise is very heavy and requires almost superhuman strength and stamina to perform the violently active dances while wearing it.

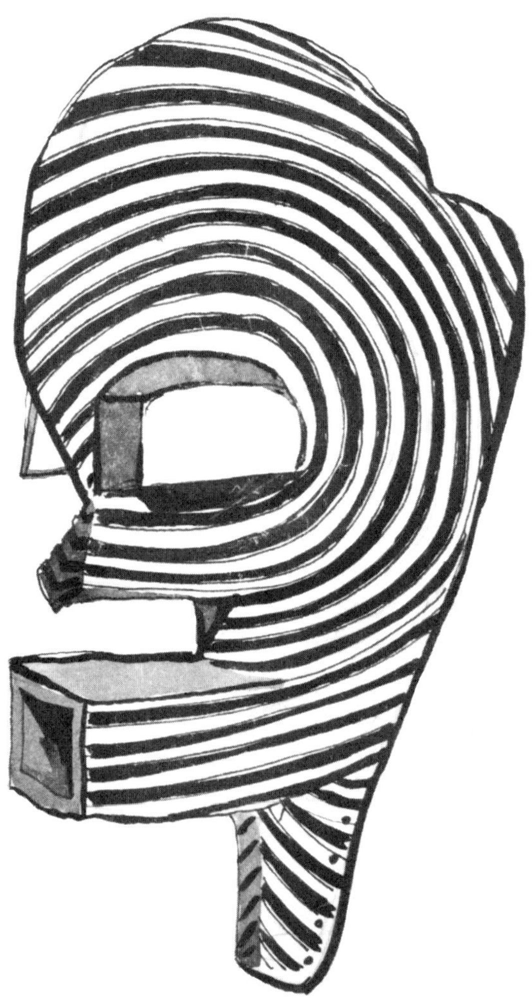

Fig. 23. Kalebue Mask. Wood. Height approximately 24 inches. Zaire. Another example of abstraction. Note the exaggerated eyes and the serrated facial scarification.

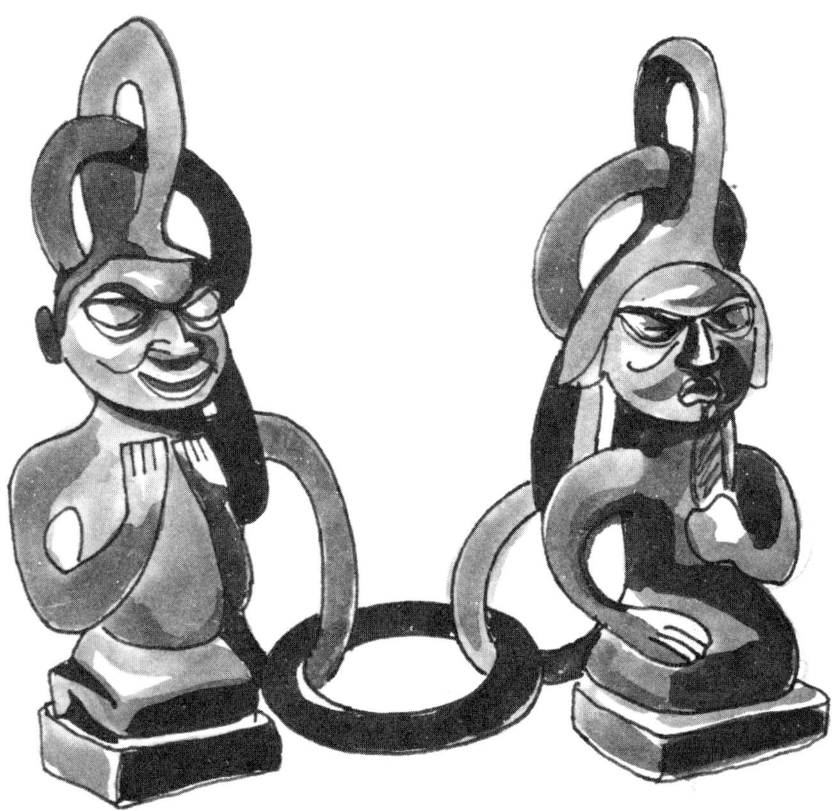

Fig. 24. Ibeji Twin Figures. Carved from one piece of wood, joined by seven chain links. Height approximately 4 or 5 inches. Yoruba, Nigeria. The male figure is usually depicted smoking a pipe. Used in rituals to insure the health of twins; if the twins die the mother carries the images in her skirt band.

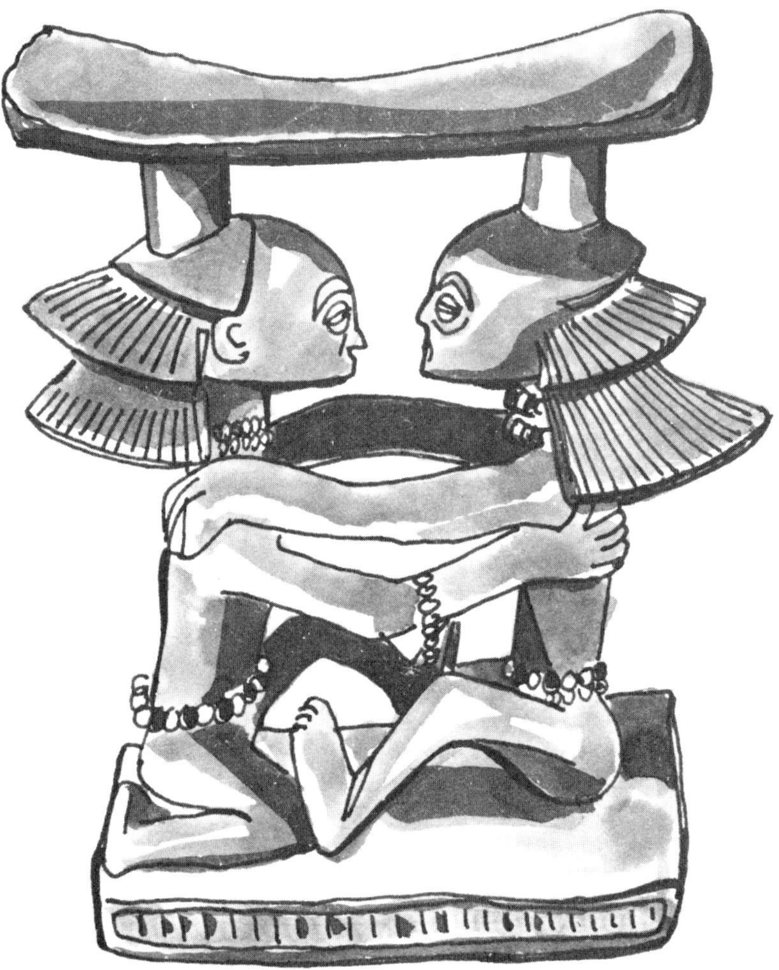

Fig. 25. Headrest. Wood and cowrie shells. Height approximately 6 inches. Stylized male/female figures. Nigeria. Note the fan-shaped elaborate hair dressing and the bead ornamentation. Such headrests were necessary to preserve hair-stylings like the ones depicted. Note the similarity to the Japanese *makura* or wood-block pillow designed for the same reason.

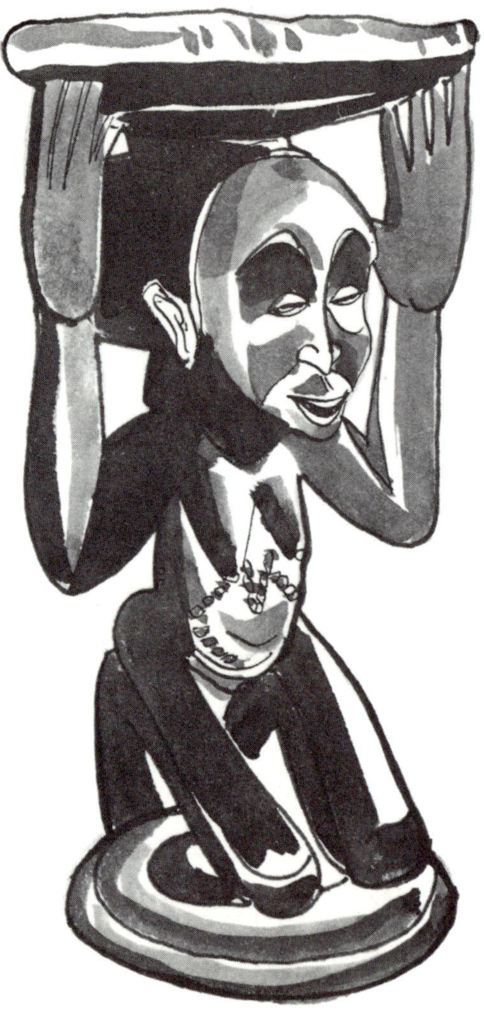

Fig. 26. Ceremonial stand. Carved wood. Height 21 inches. Baluba, Zaire. Probably used for ritual offerings. Note the naturalistic facial expression and the elaborate hair-do.

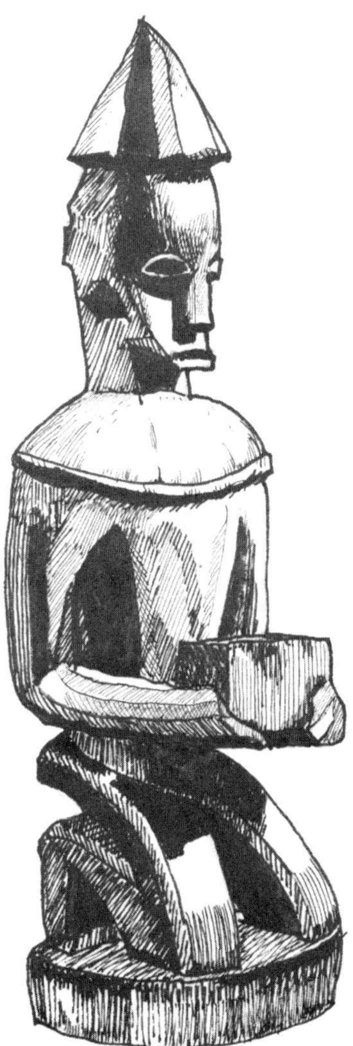

Fig. 27. Urhobo kneeling figure. Carved wood. Height approximately 26 inches Niger Delta area, Nigeria. Note the simplicity of line. Now in Museum of Primitive Art, New York.

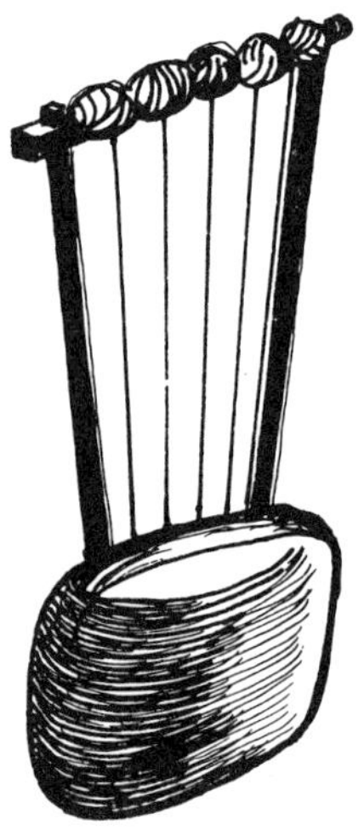

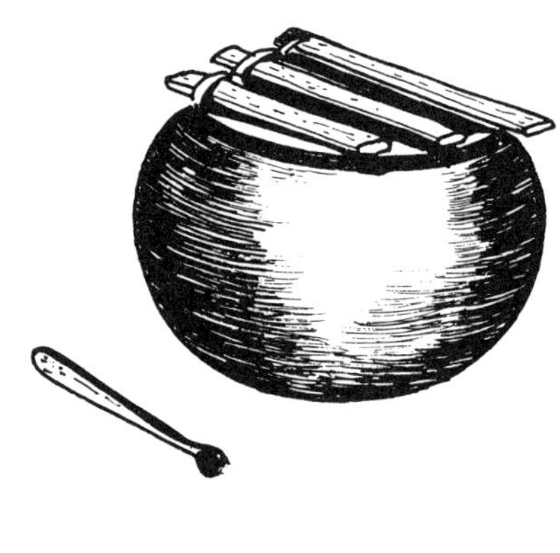

Fig. 28. Chordophone. Zaire. A simple stringed bow-harp with gourd sounding board.

Fig. 30. Xylophone. Zaire. Wooden strips of varying length laid across a gourd struck with a mallet of wood.

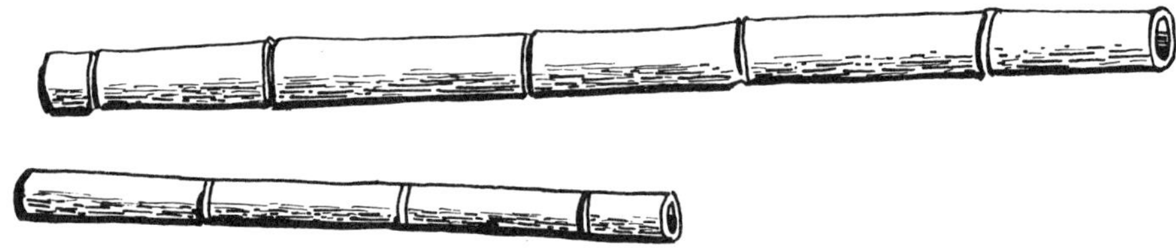

Fig. 29. Idiophones. Zaire. Long tubes of hollowed-out bamboo which produce a sound when pounded upon the ground; some are seven and eight feet long; the length and size of the tube varies the pitch of the sound.

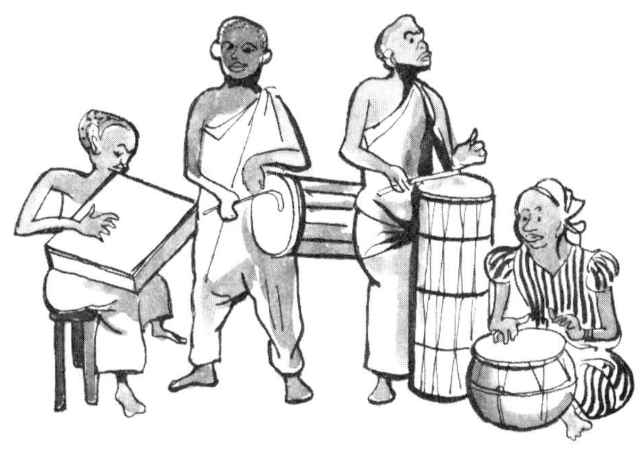

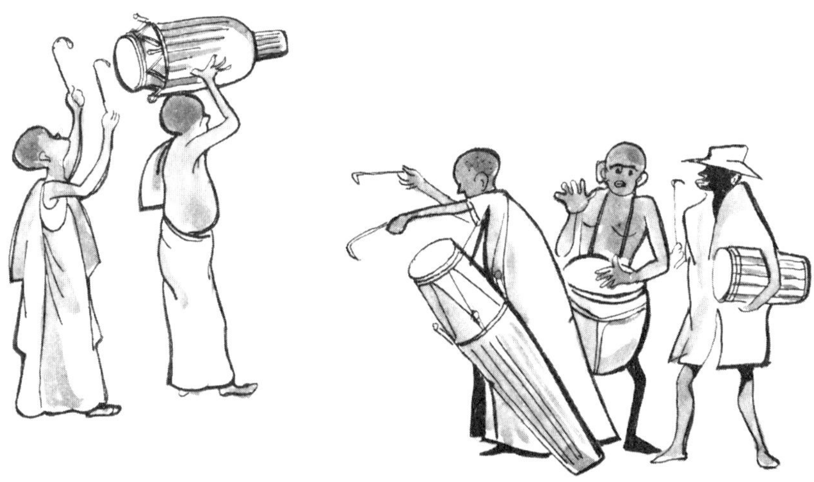

Figs. 31, 32, 33. African Drummers and Drums. The drums are of varying sizes, a few of the astonishing variety of shapes. Some ancient ceremonial drums were covered with human skin.

Contemporary Arts

A melange of the old and the new, the African, the western, and the oriental envelops much of Africa today. In the urban centers streamlined airports and luxury hotels are very much in evidence and restaurants and nightclubs, automobiles, transistor radios, television sets and air conditioners. Big cities like Legos and Ibadan, Nairobi and Mombasa, Kinshasa and Lubumbashi offer every modern convenience and many of the distractions and also the inevitable pollution of twentieth century mechanized society.

In Africa a well-to-do middle class group vies with young intellectuals in the university centers and elsewhere in advocating and displaying the latest European and American imports. Even in the villages, "upstair houses" overshadow many of the ancient low-slung mud and plaster structures which in their own unpretentious way seem frequently much more artistically attractive than the modern buildings. Movies and cola drinks and jukebox jazz abound; western recording stars compete for popularity with any number of local groups and combos which have quickly caught on to the latest fads in music.

But the rhythms of the traditional drumming continue, and some of the traditional dancing. All over Africa there are festivals celebrated by one group or another in honor of one of the age-old gods—Ogun, God of War and Iron, in Nigeria, for instance, or Shango, God of Thunder. Some dedicated believers perform the old rituals with knowledge and understanding; many others participate on the edges, for the feasting and the gaiety. There are masqueraders and feats of magic and demonstrations of superhuman strength. Some of the masks worn are venerated as sacred and serious; some are intended to be satirical and amusing, making fun of local officials or dignitaries as well as the peculiarities of foreigners. Religion in Africa may be less clearly defined and more universally accepted as a part of daily life than elsewhere; more diversified, perhaps. Many different manifestations of religion are tolerated and accepted with their distinctive rituals, trappings and ceremonials. There is laughter and song and enjoyable release as well as serious worship.

Nigeria

Masquerade societies exist in Nigeria, such as the Gelede (for women only), which uses songs and dances to exorcise witches, and the Gyungun or Agbegijo (for men), designed to appease and to worship ancestors. Some of the song-dance-ritual may be similar in form to the dithyrambs of the ancient Greeks in celebrations for the God Dionysus, which, according to tradition, produced Thespis, the first actor, and led toward the development of Greek tragic drama. Such a cultural parallel is conjecture, but the analogy may be entirely feasible.

The professional Yoruba-language theatre may have started with Hubert Ogunde, an actor-playwright-poet, who used Christian Bible stories like that of Nebuchadnezzer and the Garden of Eden as well as traditional Yoruba legends and folklore as subject matter for his plays. Ogunde's plays include *The Yoruba Rover, Black Forest, Love of Money,* and quite recently an adaptation of the medieval morality play *Everyman.*

Currently professional theatre thrives in Nigeria. A recurring contemporary theme, quite naturally, concerns the conflict of cultures and problems in adapting the traditional with the modern, the African with the Western. Many professional companies regularly perform the plays of professional playwrights like Wole Soyinka (*The Swamp Dwellers, The Lion and the Jewel, A Dance of the Forests*) and John Pepper Clark (*The Masquerade, The Raft, The Song of the Goat*). Amateur groups flourish, particularly those connected with the universities. Not long ago a group of students and teachers from the University of Ibadan took plays, including cut-down versions of Shakespeare, out into the remote areas and performed before audiences of tribesmen and villagers who had never previously seen any kind of formal theatre, much less ever heard of Shakespeare. The audiences loved it and asked for more! The theatre, like music, has universal appeal, even when the language is not well understood.

Contemporary Nigerians increasingly achieve critical literary acclaim: the work of Wole Soyinka, poet and novelist as well as playwright, and Chinua Achebe (*The Arrow of God, No Longer at Ease, Things Fall Apart*) are becoming well known in the United States. The caustic comment of John Pepper Clark, following his study at Princeton University, in *America, Their America,* is an example of literate African protest. Other Nigerian writers receiving contemporary recognition both in and out of Africa include Cyprian Ekwensi (*Jagua Nana, People of the City, The Burning Grass*), Gabriel Okara (*The Voice*), Christopher Okigbo (*Labyrinths with Paths of Thunder*), and Niyi Oniororu (*Lagos is a Wicked Place, No More a Minister*).

In the University town of Ibadan in the Western State of Nigeria stands a reconstructed village "Mbari," or ritual house, with colorful murals painted on the exterior walls. The murals are by contemporaries but they reflect the style of ancient times with fantastic palm trees against pink backgrounds and enormous serpents and mermaids and crocodiles. On the front porch of this twentieth-century version of an ancient Mbari, an "in group" of Nigerian artists and writers gather for informal meetings. (1) The Mbari here is an artists' clubhouse. It was established in 1961 by a group of young writers, including Wole Soyinka and John Pepper Clark, Christopher Okigbo and Ezekial Mphahlele. Supported by funds derived from membership fees, the Mbari Club operates outside the government, sponsored in part by the Congress for Cultural Freedom with headquarters in Paris.

The Ibadan Mbari Club encourages and sponsors art exhibits by its membership artists and also exhibitions of works by non-Nigerians. There are programs of traditional Nigerian dancing and of traditional Nigerian music, as well as an annual Jazz Festival. The Club produces performances of operas and cantatas based upon Nigerian history and legend; it serves as a kind of clearing house and publisher for short stories and dramatic works. In 1961 it operated a summer school under the direction of Mr. Julian Bernart, an architect-teacher from South Africa; a janitor, a professor's wife, a garage attendant, a woman doctor, as well as school children attended. (2).

This original Mbari Club inspired the organization of others, and there are currently several operating throughout Nigeria. A particularly successful Mbari was established in the large western town of Oshogbo by Duro Ladipo, a Yoruba primary school teacher who is also an aspiring musician and composer, and Ulli Beier, formerly tutor in the Department of Extra-Mural Studies of the University of Ibadan. At the Oshogbo Mbari several musical dramas were successfully produced, in addition to performances of Ladipo's Easter Cantata (which had originally been composed for the church but because of the rather unorthodox use of drums had caused controversy). The Mbari Club provided an ideal location for more extensive public performances. Here also both workshop space and training classes were available. In the summer of 1964 Georgiana Beier conducted a school which ran for several seasons. She helped to train and to sponsor a number of notable artists, including Twins Seven Seven (the peculiar name was his own idea; his sketches and drawings also reflect his highly unusual inventiveness and imagination), Muraina Oyelami, Adebisi Fabunmi and Jimoh Buraimoh.

To western ears the names of these African artists sound strange and to western eyes some of their work looks nightmarishly odd! "Anti-Bird Ghost," by Twin Seven Seven, shows monsters with a multitude of elongated eyes, tiny fore-shortened legs and an arm from which grows a second head; Oyelami's "Forest Spirit" is done with blocks and cubes; Fabunmi's "Metamorphoses" reveals a purple head emphasizing a single enormous eye out of which grows a hand; and Buraimoh's "Bead Work on Cloth" shows three stylized masks in reds and browns and greens.

Speaking of her venture, Georgiana Beier wrote:

The summer school opened at 8:00 a.m. and by lunch time one was already overwhelmed by the swarming talents—ideas as numerous as leaves on a tree. The immediate problem was to recognize each person's individual possibilities at the earliest stage and confirm them in his own direction. The most incredible thing about it was that these young men wandered into the summer school with no particular purpose—perhaps mostly because it was free and they had nothing else to do. None of them was there because he had the urgent impulse to become a painter; yet not a single dull picture was created. Everybody put down confident images with sure strokes. Composition and color sense came naturally to them. It was difficult to sift the richer from the rich, the stronger from the strong. At first I was worried that a "style" might develop, and everybody might turn out the same stuff in the end. But there was in fact too much individuality from the start. (3)

Such activities are not unique in contemporary Africa where the roots of civilization are deep and great potential for art exists as yet not fully realized. Insurgency and independence have resulted in a kind of artistic renaissance. There emerges a genuine concern to rediscover the traditional arts and to find suitable security for their preservation and display in museums like the one initiated in 1927 by Mr. Kenneth Murray in Lagos. Mr. Murray was at that time an Education Officer under the British Government. Largely through his efforts a sizeable collection of Ife statues and Benin bronzes was collected and placed on display. (4) The Museum of Nigerian Antiquities, Traditional Art and

Ethnology is today the official title of the museum. Here Nigerians are being trained to take over staff positions in the work of securing artifacts and preparing them for display.

There is also in Nigeria increasing recognition of the importance of encouraging native African artistic expression, to train, instruct and provide materials and financial assistance for promising young native artists. At the museums such people can study traditional art forms and some of the exhibits are taken out for traveling displays to rural regions outside Lagos. (5)

Although many of the contemporary wood carvers in Nigeria and elsewhere have succumbed to the lathe and other machinery and tools for mass production, there still exist carvers of the old school who conform to the old patterns and use only the simplest of traditional tools [Fig. 27]. The twin male-and-female Ibeji carvings [Fig. 24], for the cult of twins societies, are produced by traditional carvers using traditional techniques.

Concerning the art of the contemporary Yoruba wood carver, Ulli Beier writes:

Even now after the countryside has been plundered by thieves (in the pay of European traders) and by more respectable but no less ruthless museum collectors, there are still innumerable carvings in use. They usually represent worshippers and priests of the gods, and less often the gods themselves. These Yoruba carvings are less abstracted than, say, Ibo masks or Senufo figures. The basic forms of this art are naturalistic. There is considerable anatomical detail: a face has cheekbones, eyelashes, earlobes and other details usually omitted in the more geometric African styles. But the naturalistic forms are adapted and distorted to suit the carver's mood and expression. The head, seat of the spirit, is extremely large, sometimes one fourth of the body. The eyes swell out from the head and can even be hemispheres stuck on to the head. The ears are set far back on the head and may not even be visible from the front. The lips are simplified to two parallel lines. The forms of a Yoruba carving appear to be produced by a kind of pressure from within: forehead, eyes, breasts and belly are all pushed outwards and the surface of the figure has the tension of a blown up balloon.

The figures are static, the weight is evenly distributed on the short legs. The carver works the front, the back and the two sides, there is no twist anywhere in the body's axis. Yet a kind of inner tension is produced, resulting from the contrast in textures and proportions, in the degree of naturalization and stylization. The basic form usually has a smooth surface like a pebble, but hairstyle, eyelashes, pubic hair and tribal markings are impressed with deep, sharp incisions. The naturalistic detail of the eye, for example, contrasts with the set of parallel lines that hint at the toes, or with the combination of triangles representing the ear. The figures are calm, but not relaxed. There is a mood of receptiveness, and often a feeling of intense concentration.

Reliefs on palace doors can be illustrative and decorative. However, the figure carvings in the shrines of orisha, which form the bulk of the artistic output of the Yoruba people, are anything but literary. They represent human beings, men and women, they explore a particular mood in infinite variations of style—but they refrain from telling stories and usually the identity of the carvers is unknown and appears to be of little interest to the worshippers. (6)

The University of Ibadan, in addition to helping sponsor the Mbari Clubs, offers degrees in Fine Arts. Other schools of higher learning offering such degrees are the University of Nigeria at Maukka in the Eastern State (patterned after the American university system) and the Nigerian Art School at Zaria in the Muslim populated north. Ulli Beier criticizes the site of Zaria as a poor location for an art school because wood is not available there for carving. He notes, however, that many of Nigeria's best contemporary artists have received training here. (7)

A Methodist sponsored college at Uzilkoli likewise encourages student practice in the arts of painting and wood carving and in the practical crafts of furniture making. Famous in Nigeria is Catholic Father Caroll's workshop at Oye-Ekili where the apprentice training method has been developed. Students fill commissions to construct modern creches, and to design church windows and carved doors. (8)

The Ibo people have traditionally been builders of elaborate spirit houses, makers of unbaked clay figures realistically fashioned and of wood carvings and masks—some delicate and attractive, some heavy and grotesque. Originally the Ibo artifacts, like most African art, were used in religious or magical rites and kept hidden from view. Modern Ibo artists—sculptors and painters trained in the family crafts—currently copy the traditional masks and figures, sometimes decorating them elaborately with polychromic color, and they bring them to the urban centers for sale to people who wish them for decorative purposes. Evidence again of the changing times and the increasingly "secularization" and professionalism in contemporary African art.

In a similar manner Yoruba peoples continue to make wood carvings and to decorate them with multicolored designs in paint and beads—carvings that were originally designed for fecundity rites. They fashion clubs with elaborate carvings, which were originally symbols in dance-drama, paired statuettes of "Ibeji" (the twin Gods of creation) [Fig. 24], ivory objects and door shutters, and sell them to tourists. These objects are made after the style and the fashion of the traditional but their use becomes today largely decorative. (9)

Perhaps the largest number of contemporary artists in Nigeria started under the guidance of Yoruba Chief Aina Onabolu, a crusader for the teaching of painting and drawing in the schools. Yemi Bisiri still works with traditional subjects in brass, using the age-old lost wax process. In striking contrast, Ovia Idah has chosen to work in concrete and cement, creating totally unique and individually eccentric work; in his late seventies he created a series of terra cotta reliefs, weirdly designed and emotionally disturbing.

Ben Enwonwu, another Yoruba painter and sculptor, studied in England in the 1940's and became a Federal Arts Adviser. Enwonwu painted an official portrait of Queen Elizabeth. (10)

Whereas the peoples of southern and western Nigeria were traditionally beaters of drums, the northern peoples were blowers of horns. Today the Hausa in the north construct elaborate horns and decorate them lavishly. The Hausa also produce fine leather work, embroidery, and weaving; their materials include banana leaves and raffia. Some designs are colored red with dye made from roots, but characteristic is the Indigo blue—a brilliant and vivid hue which predominates in Hausa art.

In the northern Nigerian city of Abuja everyone seems to be a potter. Here almost unlimited resources of firewood, water and clay, the raw materials necessary, and a traditional skill exist. Pottery is further encouraged by a Pottery Training Center which is sponsored in large part by the Northern Regional Government. (11) Under the direction of staff members, students learn to perfect their craft. Many come from surrounding villages or rural regions to learn and then return to their native areas to produce ceramic ware. Some of the techniques of glazing and design are foreign and contemporary, but the teachers at Abuja conscientiously try to avoid the danger of a foreign design and technique overshadowing the native and the traditional. Women originally were the potters—there was a tradition that men who worked at the pottery never got married!—but the trend today is toward male potters. It is they who develop the new forms while the women generally follow the old techniques of modeling the pots by building up layer after layer of clay coiled into ropelike lengths. The designs on Hausa pottery tend to be abstract and nonrepresentational.

Typical among the more than sixty-two contemporary artists listed by the Harmon Foundation Study of African Contemporary Art and Artists is Ladi Kawali, who was born thirty miles south of Abuja in the southern part of the Northwestern State. Kawali fashions handsome water jars, molding the clay and building layer upon layer. She decorates the pots with incised designs of lizards and crocodiles. Occasionally she uses a potter's wheel to make (or "to throw") beakers and cups. These she later decorates with white inlay worked under a dark glaze. Kawali has demonstrated her work in England, in West Germany, Switzerland and quite recently in the United States.

Another Nigerian artist is a man named Bamgboye who is considered one of the best of the surviving Yoruba traditional carvers. Using a sharp adz, a knife and a few chisels, he makes stools and trays decorated with conventionalized pictures of cowrie shells, birds' eyes and portions of other animals. He never carves human portraits. Although very old, he continues to do superb work. However, the brilliance is lacking when he does a job on consignment or commission. His carving depends largely upon his inspiration.

KENYA

Many of the "Afro art objects" which clutter the counters of gift shops in America—the crudely fashioned wood carvings of antelope twins or triplets or fatbellied figurines or big sharp-featured heads festooned with bits of feather and beads, as well as some rather skillfully fashioned and cleverly designed earrings made from shell or bits of twisted wire supporting curious seed pods, some of them brilliantly dyed—many of these "Afro objects" come from Kenya.

Kenya also does land-office business in tourist trade. There has developed what the Kenya artists refer to as "airport pop art"—and it's a profitable business. But most of these objects are quickly fashioned for quantity rather than quality; only relatively few may be considered truly artistic. Unfortunately also, handcrafting begins to give way to machine production and materials like plastics begin to replace the native woods and shells and beads.

Contemporary primitive tribal groups like the Masai have always been nomadic hunters and warriors with little use for or perhaps interest in encumbering art objects. But the Masai have traditionally decorated their shields, and with the influx of tourists they construct leather shields and emboss them with geometric designs from their traditional past, sometimes coloring the designs, and sell them as souvenirs to tourists [Fig. 34]. The Kikuyu and the Akamba tribes are making and selling certain versions of the clay male and female figures which were used traditionally in harvest ritual ceremonies. (12) Characteristic are the protruding umbilicus of the male figures and the triangular apron of the female figures. The aprons are sometimes decorated with blue beads.

Among the Bantu peoples of central Kenya utility objects, like wooden vessels and clay pots, are usually decorated with geometric designs or with schematic abstract figures of men, animals and plants, of moons, stars, arrows, and snakes. (13) Dark turquoise and pink beads are reserved for the decorations of the chiefs as a mark of status.

Some of the pots have lugs on the sides which are pierced with holes so that a strap or thong can be introduced through the lugs. The pot can then be carried on the back, supported and balanced by the thong across the forehead. Typical of Bantu pottery from ancient times as well as modern is the technique of building up the shape by coiling or "roping" with clay.

The Bantu peoples also make and sell various kinds of calabashes [Fig. 7]. These are vessels made from hollowed-out gourds of various shapes and sizes; the highly polished surfaces are incised with decorative designs, usually geometric, sometimes with color rubbed in. The calabashes are prized as souvenirs by tourists and native Africans alike. They are useful as practical containers but they are also ornamental.

Tomb ornaments, funeral posts, and commemorative totem poles with carvings of the deceased—fairly realistic and with typically regional features and facial markings—are fashioned by the Bantu people after the manner of their forebears [Fig. 6]. But among the Bantu of central Kenya little carving is done. Around the Kilimanjaro district, natives mold clay figures called "nungu" and they fashion pots for funeral ceremonies called "vigango," which are elaborately carved in geometric designs for the most part but with some abstract male-female figures. (14) In this region the Kenyan natives paint their walls with mythical religious pictures or two-headed monsters, with snakes and crocodiles, rather similar to those of the Nigerian Mbari houses.

To preserve native and traditional Kenyan art the Corydon Museum at Nairobi was started in 1915, largely as an archaeological museum. Some originals, but mostly plaster replicas in imitation of the

Bushman paintings, are stored and displayed there. There are decorative shields, basketry fashioned by nomadic tribes, earrings of the Wakamba and the Kishii. The Corydon Museum has since become the National Museum of Kenya. Its collection of native art objects increases yearly.

University College in Nairobi (started in 1956) conducts classes in painting and in life-drawing. Some critics have felt the methods and styles taught are too European. They feel the need for concerted effort to dig back into tradition and encourage native design. (15)

Started about 1956, also, the Kenya Design School studies the designs of nomadic tribes, particularly the shield decorations and the carved ivories and the calabashes. In 1966, the Kenya National Art Foundation was established with the objective of fostering and preserving native artistic expression.

In Kenya there is great potential for more artistic expression, freed from tradition on the one hand and from the influences of foreign cultures on the other; it could develop into a significant and original native art. These contemporary artists of Kenya typify this potential:

James Bukhala (Ashiono) makes use of banana fibers in painting. He also makes sculptures in wood or clay. He toured the United States, attended Syracuse University, and returned as a teacher of art to Kenya. A member of the M'Luyia tribe, he was born in Kenya in 1932.

Francis Ndegun, a member of the Kikuyu tribe, was born in 1924. He spent his early life herding sheep and goats and he walked thirty miles to a Catholic mission school. He had his first drawing lesson at twenty. He stayed at school long enough to graduate from the Makerere School of Art, where he later taught painting and simple folk arts. In the early days when he had no money at all, he used colored juices from flowers or anything at all he could make a mark with.

Gregory Maloba of the Mulyia tribe was born in 1922; a graduate of the School of Art at Makerere College, he later went to England and studied at the University of Bristol and at the Royal College of Art in London. Here, of course, he absorbed many western ideas and techniques and methods. He works in stone, bronze, cement, and terra cotta. He exhibits his work in private collections. While he was in Bristol he held a one-man show and presented his figure, called "Compassion" to Princess Margaret of England.

Mwenze (Kibwanga) is a Masai who was born in 1930. His favorite subjects are human beings depicted in violent action or struggling against tremendous forces. His work has been shown both in the Netherlands and in London.

As in almost every other country in the world, in Kenya today the Western motion picture and TV is popular in urban areas (and bit by bit they appear even in rural and more remote areas). There are occasional imports of Western formal theatre. Very little natively produced professional theatre exists currently in Kenya, although some university centers have drama or play production groups reflecting British traditions. Recently in Kenya several Drama Festivals have offered prizes to encourage playwriting.

University idealists and some of the prosperous middle class businessmen are presently interested in rediscovering and reviving traditional African music and dancing. And at the festivals and ceremonials, traditions in these arts persist outside the large cities.

Increasingly new writers are emerging in Kenya to make their comment—to describe, to advocate or to protest and to entertain. A favorite theme here too evolves around the problems of tribal or inter-racial adjustment to modern customs and ways.

Among the contempoary writers, natives of Kenya, who have published work of literary merit in English (or who have been translated into English) are these: James Ngugi (*The Black Hermit, A Grain of Wheat, Weep Not Child, The Fig Tree*), Grace Ogot (*Takayo* and other short stories, *The Promised Land, Land Without Thunder*), Marina Gashe (*The Village, The Scar*), J. Gatanya (*The Battlefield*), L. Kibera and S. Kahiaga (*The Potent Ash: Short Stories*), Henry Olela (*Beyond Those Hills*), Nassir Ben Juma Bhalo (*Poems from Kenya—Gnomic Verse in Swahili*), L. Okola (ed.) (*Drum Beat*), O. Pibitek (*Song of Lawino: A Lament*), and G. Wachire (*Ordeal in the Forest*).

There are many other contemporary Kenyan writers in several languages and in several fields other than "literature": in economics, political science, and philosophy, for instance. And increasingly a considerable amount of critical commentary by foreigners about Kenya, descriptions of one sort or another, or stories centering about the region are reaching western markets. There is the fascinating account of Joy Adamson, made into a film, entitled *Born Free,* and, among travel books with a literary turn, Ilka Chase's amusing but authentic account entitled *The Elephants Arrive at Half Past Five.* And somewhat earlier there were the fascinating stories about her life on an African estate in Kenya by the late Isak Dinesen.

ZAIRE

Independence and the influx of foreign tourists have made the art of the Republic of Zaire popular. Today the government makes every effort to prevent the destruction of cultural remains of the past. Traditional arts, instruments of agriculture from ancient times, historical sites, as well as the protection and the display of artifacts both ancient and modern, are the nationally sponsored responsibility of some fourteen museums around the country. (16) Large collections of masks, fetish figures, carved benches and cup-bearing figures are included in the fine displays of Kinshasa and particularly in the Art Museum at Mushenge [Fig. 21-23; 26].

In the "applied arts" or crafts, basketry and weaving abound in modern Zaire; craftsmen (and women) use centuries old methods and incorporate ancient designs together with the modern [Fig. 35]. The designs are largely geometrical shapes—borders of crossed lines, triangles, interlocking squares, some of them rubbed with stain to add color. Handles of scepters used by judges, or fly switches, cups, combs and musical instruments may bear carvings of human heads or figures and, more rarely, animals. These are primarily decorative or ornamental, but perhaps some represent talismen or lucky symbols. Among the characteristic Zarien domestic ware are jars with long necks decorated with figures of birds and humans and vessels or vases in the shape of human figures, some of them garbed in Western style.

At each of the three universities, particularly at the University of Kinshasa Academy of Fine Arts and at the Academy of Design at Lubumbashi, instruction is given in painting, sculpture, ceramics, and architecture. The revival of Zarien sculpture stems from a study of the four regional or traditional styles: the Bandundu, the Kasi, the Northeastern and the Northwestern. Some of the characteristic creative work of each of these is given in the pages covering traditional arts of Africa in an earlier section of this study. The materials employed are mostly wood and ivory, but various modern materials and techniques are also beginning to be used—such as embossed copperplate, stone engraving and concrete work.

According to the official *Guide to the Democratic Republic of the Congo,* painting was first introduced in 1908. The first native artist to paint was Lunaki who exhibited in the Ethnological Museum at Geneva. (17) Since that time the art of painting has spread through the country and today there are hundreds of painters who are graduates of specialized art schools or who have been trained by foreigners.

Ceramics is a growing medium; modern technical methods gradually replaced the traditional "open-sky" cooking, and modern kilns and furnaces are used. Embossed copper is in vogue mostly in Lubumbashi.

Among the contemporary Congolese artists listed in the Harmon Foundation report as presently creating in the Republic of Zaire are:

Joseph Kabongo, a member of the Bakwatembo-Dibaya tribe, who paints patterns of colored lines and dots—rather like the pointillist style of European nineteenth-century artists. An honor graduate in 1958 of the Academie des Beaux-Arts at Elizabethville, he traveled in Germany and exhibited there in 1960-61 three paintings of mythological animals.

Jean Luvwezo, who came from Zaire in the fall of 1960 to Princeton

University as an Economics and Political Science major on a four-year scholarship from the African-American Institute. He is a self-taught artist, encouraged by Jean Vanden Bossche, who was Director of the Museum at Leopoldville (now Kinshasa). He watched and then copied European and native African painters. He was encouraged by Bossche to work in the original style he has since developed. He has had one man shows in New York as well as in Zaire.

Pili Pili Mulongoya, a graduate of the Congo Academy of Folk Art. He got his start working as a car washer for Romain-Desfosses, who founded the school. He has developed a type of decorative painting inspired by nature studies. Animals and vegetables are his favorite subjects. Three of his paintings exhibited in New York are entitled "Snake Amid Flowers," "Crocodile Eating Fish," and "Eagle Attacking Deer."

Even during the periods of foreign occupation exceptionally talented students went abroad to study and today even more students from Zaire, many of them sponsored in part by the government, go abroad to study. They bring to the foreign country—whether Belgium, the United States, Italy, France or England—new understandings and new vitality from Africa. They return with expanded horizons and new viewpoints. If they are writers their work consciously or unconsciously reflects their experience. The work of the patriot Patrice Lumumba entitled *Congo, My Country* has been translated and widely circulated; less well known but of considerable literary merit is the work of A. Cesaire called *Return to My Native Land* and *Une Saison au Congo.*

Many visitors refer to the Republic of Zaire as a "musical paradise." Tourists arriving at Kinshasa are struck by the festival atmosphere of this capital city. Drummers abound—even performing on street corners —and the sound of radios at high volume transmitting music of the rhumba and the Cha-cha intermingle with less easily recognizable, but clearly rhythmic and exciting, sounds. There are eight nationally recognized professional orchestral groups in Kinshasa. And there are five big theatrical troupes as well as nine government sponsored folkloric societies set up to answer "the call of our government to revive our customs, our songs and dances." (18) Several amateur theatrical groups in the capital city of Kinshasa—like the Theatre of the Twelve, The African Theatrical Union, The Theatre of the Three Negroes—produce regularly in the Zoo Theatre and entertain from time to time in the interior of the country.

The contemporary artistic scene in Nigeria, Kenya, and the Republic of Zaire reveals an admixture of the native African and the foreign, the ancient and the modern, the professional and the amateur, the skillful and the inartistic. Evidence points to a great potential of artistic expression becoming increasingly aesthetic rather than functional, and perhaps more universal than ethnocentric.

Summary

Many of the traditional artist-craftsmen of Africa have become carpenters, or producers of inferior "Pop Art," or forgers of antiques for the tourist trade. Machine-made or partially machine-made products clutter local native markets; imports replace the old-fashioned calabash, and cotton materials machine-woven in England replace hand-loomed cloth; plastics replace pottery. In this respect Africa, like every other part of the world, seems destined to be bogged down eventually with a kind of pseudo-Western-contemporary culture—a kind of mass produced synthetic amalgamation!

In other respects, however, the mixture of foreign ideas and techniques has revitalized some African artists. Ulli Beir points out:

The African artist has refused to be fossilized. New types of artists give expression to new ideas, work for different clients, fulfill new functions. Accepting the challenge of Europe, the African artist does not hesitate to adopt new materials, be inspired by foreign art, look for a different role in society. New forms, new styles and new personalities are emerging everywhere and this contemporary African art is rapidly becoming as rich and as varied as were the more rigid artistic conventions of several generations ago. (19)

The modern African artist no longer works entirely within the framework of the religious or the ceremonial traditions of his ancestors, and his work no longer is entirely conceptual and functional. But memories and dreams creep into his consciousness from his childhood or from the legends he has heard from his elders—and these influence him. The tradition of creative art as bound up with function—with the ritual, the ceremony—persists just beneath the surface of his mind.

On festival days—although perhaps planned largely for the edification and entertainment of the tourists and the foreigners, and for profit —he may participate in the dances and the chanting, help with the drumming and the hand clapping. He may contribute a mask carving or a ceremonial headdress or paint his body in the traditional manner of his ancestors. And he may do so with laughter and bantering, and with very little knowledge of the secret rites involved, without much interest in them, and surely not with complete belief or faith in the ritual.

But he does participate. Some of the "magic" of the ceremonial rubs off on him despite his modern sophistication. A form of empathy occurs. He will shout and laugh and be amused and entertained as he entertains others, but the rhythms and the words of the chants, the texture of the garments he wears and the sight of the symbols he carries may affect him, enter his soul, and provide him with identity.

Contemporary African Writing

Writers native to Africa are making significant contributions to literature in plays and novels, short stories and poems, as well as essays and editorial comment in magazines and newspapers. Many Africans are writing in English, which is to them a secondary language; those writing in other languages are having their work translated into English. An undercurrent of regional heritage which may reflect an experience specifically African may be evident in some of the writing; there are also evidences of a universal concern for humanity that is neither regional nor contemporary. Although some of the selections here are excerpts and only a very few selections are included, they are perhaps a meaningful sampling of much wider range in subject matter and techniques which is currently African.

The Cup Was Full

C.O.D. EKWENSI

Trained in pharmacy in London, Cyprian Ekwensi, a native Ibo, served as Director of Information Services for the Nigerian Government. In addition to his published short stories, Ekwensi is the author of three published novels: *People of the City* (1953); *Jagua Nana* (1961); and *Burning Grass* (1962).

Bolarin was not happy. His face was spotted, his mouth tasted lousy, and there were rings of sleepiness under his dull red eyes. Whatever it was that worried him, did not seem to be known to his wives, for they went about their household duties, ever conscious of that jealousy that is inseparable from the private life of a polygamist.

One of them came to Bolarin, knelt down and handed him his palm wine. He accepted it mechanically, not because Aina was his favourite wife but because he felt it was a good thing to bury his sorrows in drink, to try to forget. . . .

But how could he, when every dawn brought the time nearer? How could he forget when a thousand little things reminded him of it? He stared fixedly before him but he wasn't seeing the goats, or the bananas, or the palm tree in his compound. He was seeing the past.

He saw himself as the Oba's right-hand man, a position which brought him in contact with influential men, and enabled him to make quite an appreciable sum on his own. Things had gone without a hitch. He married wives, he had cocoa farms, he had established lorry transport of his own. Until six days ago, life was worth something to him; but now, the Oba was dead, and he knew he also had to follow suit.

Bolarin emptied the wine at a gulp and wiped his moustaches with the back of his hand. He was still seated in the couch staring dully into the compound. The clouds were gathering and he imagined it was coming on to rain.

He didn't like to think of it. He didn't want them to know he was— well, afraid? That was putting it a little bluntly. If they knew—or even guessed that he wasn't an ardent supporter of fantastic traditions, they would murder him; and without any scruples either.

He had been to school. He had read quite a bit. Bolarin in his twenty-seven years' experience of life had never been able to understand why one man should lay down his life simply because his superior had lost his. The old Oba dead. Let him go!

Bolarin stood up—a big man in whose rounded arms and gorgeous *lappa* you could see wealth, and the effects of lazy living. It was in moments like this that he generally sought the company of Ayoke. He went indoors, put on his *bubu* around those massive shoulders, hid his bald head with a *fila,* and left the room.

'I am going,' he told his wives.

A chorus of good wishes answered him.

The weather continued to be gloomy but he could see his way through the alleys and by-paths of the village. The quietness of the deserted streets seemed to harmonize with his present mood, and presently he stopped before one of the thatched low mud buildings, called out the traditional *ekale-o!*, and went in.

She was seated on the bed, just fresh from her bath. A tiny mirror was propped between her knees and she was doing her hair. Bolarin looked at this tall slim girl with the glowing olive-tinted shoulders, and his pulse quickened.

The smile she bestowed on him, the curtsy, the embarrassment she felt at his presence—all combined to make him feel fussed up and out of place. He sank into the deck-chair, thinking: 'I've often wanted to marry this girl, and each time she has put me off. Now it is too late.'

It was awkward sitting there in the semi-darkness, saying nothing, doing nothing, but he derived a certain confidence from her presence, and he was afraid to break it by talking.

'There's some big trouble on,' he muttered at last.

'Oh,' she said, looking interested.

'Don't tell anyone,' he confided and their eyes met. She lowered hers, liquid black and brilliant in the half-light.

'Please don't tell me,' she begged, 'if it's a secret.'

'It is. Women are not supposed to know. But', he drew a deep breath, 'I can't help it. You must know—' and he poured out the tale to her.

'You know he died six nights ago,' he concluded, 'which means that everything must end tomorrow night.'

She came and sat on the arm of his chair, but turned her eyes from him.

'I've given away my lands and things. There's some money I've left for you, but I want to give you something substantial, something you can look back on when I'm gone and say: "Bolarin gave this to me".'

'I don't want anything,' she said.

'That's not possible,' he said, holding her close. He felt the softness of her womanhood and cursed his fate.

The room was growing dark, but he did not ask her to light up.

'I wish I hadn't known you,' she said.

So they sat for a long while, he in the deck-chair and she on the arm, and when at last he left, his temporary comfort was gone.

In the evening of the following day the dummers came to the compound. Chairs were put out in a horse-shoe formation, and there were festivities from sunset till well past midnight. The women were in their best clothes—arsenals of gold, lace, and velvet. Drinks went round and the belles of the village did a hip dance to the rhythm of the drums.

And Ayoke? She was there too. Dressed in a magnificent plum-coloured velvet *buba* and waist-cloth, she looked more like the wife of an Oba than the mistress of his right-hand man.

Something in her eye made him postpone the inevitable moment again and again.

Suddenly he became conscious of someone talking to him. Someone brought a new gas lamp into the middle of the horseshoe, and for a moment everyone squinted from the powerful rays. There was a lull in the drumming and before he grasped what was happening, he was on his feet, addressing the people not without sentiment, and making large money presents to the drummer and the pretty women.

When he returned to his seat, Ayoke was gone. The thing was becoming terrifying. The faint hope that had lingered in his mind during the last seven days suddenly left him.

There was no way out of it. He was caught in a trap of superstition, tradition, custom. . . .

He knew they were watching his every moment, those old withered men in the shadows, with their shrunk bodies and toothless gums. He got up and walked out of the region of festivities towards the place in the Oba's compound. The shadows swallowed him.

It grew darker with every step, but he knew his way. His footsteps echoed back at him as he crossed the palace, and he hurried on among the huts in the palace compound, twisting and turning. Once he paused, panting, and rested his fat hand on the wall at his left. He glanced for a moment at the black sky overhead, and then continued.

Presently he came to the steps. Deliberately, he descended them. Thirty of them he reckoned. He walked a few paces forward, turned to the right. He looked back. It was completely dark, he could see nothing, but he felt certain he wasn't followed. He stumbled against the stool, and the stout hemp rope, which began swaying, swaying. . . . He shuddered to think he would soon be at the end of that rope.

He hesitated a long while before he made up his mind to mount the stool. The moment had come. He couldn't hear a sound—except his own breathing and his own heart. He couldn't tell the time or what was going on in the outside world. His hand trembled as he reached for the noose. Sweat streamed down the entire length of his body, and his *buba* gummed to his skin, restricting his movements.

He had put his head in the noose, his body was poised to upset the balance of the stool, when he stopped, gasping. He thought he had heard a noise, the faintest suggestion of a movement. He waited a second, eyes bulging, and then he wiped his wet throat, ashamed of his own nervousness. Then he braced himself for the swing.

Again, that suggestion, from the very darkness that shrouded him. But this time the hidden terrors came out of it in a body, making his blood turn chilly.

'Get down,' they shouted.

He got down. A torchlight cut into his face, hurting his eyes. The beam concentrated on his wrists and he watched the handcuffs as one of the men snapped them on.

'You're under arrest for attempted suicide,' he said.

He followed them, too speechless to ask how policemen had tracked him down into this subterranean abode of death.

When they had negotiated those endless twists and turns they stood at last in the middle of the village. The celebration had broken up, and its place was taken by a strange silence.

'Bring the girl too,' ordered one of the policemen, 'and let's go. The District Officer will be waiting.'

'The girl!' Bolarin heard the words in amazement.

'Ayoke! Was she with him still?' Then her voice came through to him, as in a dream, 'Be brave,' she was saying, 'the end of this will be good. For us both.'

Note: This story presents a kind of interesting paradox: its content is African, dealing with the breaking away from the old tribal tradition toward a new kind of freedom. Yet the form of the story is rather old-fashioned Western. It has a kind of O'Henry ending "complete with the marines arriving in the nick of time." Here is a clear example of the synthesis of two cultures.

Exile

C. ACHEBE

An Ibo from southern Nigeria, Chinua Achebe is a graduate of University College, Ibadan. He has been employed by the Nigerian Broadcasting Company for several years. This extract is from his novel *Things Fall Apart* (1958). He has also written *No Longer at Ease* (1960), and *The Arrow of God* (1967).

Go-di-di-go-go-di-go. Di-go-go-di-go. It was the *ekwe* talking to the clan. One of the things every man learned was the language of the hollowed-out wooden instrument. Diim! Diim! boomed the cannon at intervals.

The first cock had not crowed, and Umuofia was still swallowed up in sleep and silence when the *ekwe* began to talk, and the cannon shattered the silence. Men stirred on their bamboo beds and listened anxiously. Somebody was dead. The cannon seemed to rend the sky. Di-go-go-di-go-di-di-go-go floated in the message-laden night air. The faint and distant wailing of women settled like a sediment of sorrow on the earth. Now and again a full-chested lamentation rose above the wailing whenever a man came into the place of death. He raised his voice once or twice in manly sorrow and then sat down with the other men listening to the endless wailing of the women and the esoteric language of the *ekwe*. Now and again the cannon boomed. The wailing of the women would not be heard beyond the village, but the *ekwe* carried the news to all the nine villages and even beyond. It began by naming the clan: *Umuofia obodo dike,* 'the land of the brave'. *Umuofia obodo dike! Umuofia obodo dike!* It said this over and over again, and as it dwelt on it, anxiety mounted in every heart that heaved on a bamboo bed that night. Then it went nearer and named the village: *Iguedo of the yellow grinding-stone!* It was Okonkwo's village. Again and again Iguedo was called and men waited breathlessly in all the nine villages. At last the man was named and people sighed. 'E-u-u, Ezeudu is dead'. A cold shiver ran down Okonkwo's back as he remembered the last time the old man had visited him. 'That boy calls you father,' he had said. 'Bear no hand in his death.'

Ezeudu was a great man, so all the clan was at his funeral. The ancient drums of death beat, guns and cannon were fired, and men dashed about in frenzy, cutting down every tree or animal they saw, jumping over walls and dancing on the roof. It was a warrior's funeral, and from morning till night warriors came and went in their age groups. They all wore smoked raffia skirts and their bodies were painted with chalk and charcoal. Now and again an ancestral spirit or *egwugwu* appeared from the underworld, speaking in a tremulous, unearthly voice and completely covered in raffia. Some of them were very violent, and there had been a mad rush for shelter earlier in the day when when one appeared with a sharp machete and was only prevented from doing serious harm by two men who restrained him with the help of a strong rope tied around his waist. Sometimes he turned round and chased those men, and they ran for their lives. But they always returned to the long rope he trailed behind. He sang, in a terrifying voice, that Ekwensu, or Evil Spirit had entered his eye.

But the most dreaded of all was yet to come. He was always alone and was shaped like a coffin. A sickly odour hung in the air wherever he went, and flies went with him. Even the greatest medicine-men took shelter when he was near. Many years ago another *egwugwu* had dared to stand his ground before him and had been transfixed to the spot for two days. This one had only one hand and with it carried a basket full of water.

But some of the *egwugwu* were quite harmless. One of them was so old and infirm that he leaned heavily on a stick. He walked unsteadily to the place where the corpse was laid, gazed at it a while and went away again—to the underworld.

The land of the living was not far removed from the domain of the ancestors. There was coming and going between them, especially at festivals and also when an old man died, because an old man was very close to the ancestors. A man's life from birth to death was a series of transition rites which brought him nearer and nearer to his ancestors.

Ezeudu had been the oldest man in his village, and at his death there were only three men in the whole clan who were older, and four or five others in his own age group. Whenever one of these ancient men appeared in the crowd to dance unsteadily the funeral steps of the tribe, younger men gave way and the tumult subsided.

It was a great funeral, such as befitted a noble warrior. As the evening drew near, the shouting and the firing of guns, the beating of drums and the brandishing and clanging of machetes increased.

Ezeudu had taken three titles in his life. It was a rare achievement. There were only four titles in the clan, and only one or two men in any generation ever achieved the fourth and highest. When they did, they became the lords of the land. Because he had taken titles, Ezeudu was to be buried after dark with only a glowing brand to light the sacred ceremony.

But before this quiet and final rite, the tumult increased tenfold. Drums beat violently and men leaped up and down in frenzy. Guns were fired on all sides and sparks flew out as machetes clanged together in warriors' salutes. The air was full of dust and the smell of gunpowder. It was then that the one-handed spirit came, carrying a basket full of water. People made way for him on all sides and the noise subsided. Even the smell of gunpowder was swallowed in the sickly smell that now filled the air. He danced a few steps to the funeral drums and then went to see the corpse.

'Ezeudu!' he called in his guttural voice. 'If you had been poor in your last life I would have asked you to be rich when you come again. But you were rich. If you had been a coward, I would have asked you to bring courage. But you were a fearless warrior. If you had died young, I would have asked you to get life. But you lived long. So I shall ask you to come again the way you came before. If your death was the death of nature, go in peace. But if a man caused it, do not allow him a moment's rest.' He danced a few more steps and went away.

The drums and the dancing began again and reached fever-heat. Darkness was around the corner, and the burial was near. Guns fired the last salute and the cannon rent the sky. And then from the centre of the delirious fury came a cry of agony and shouts of horror. It was as if a spell had been cast. All was silent. In the centre of the crowd a boy lay in a pool of blood. It was the dead man's sixteen-year-old son, who with his brothers and half-brothers had been dancing the traditional farewell to their father. Okonkwo's gun had exploded and a piece of iron had pierced the boy's heart.

The confusion that followed was without parallel in the tradition of Umuofia. Violent deaths were frequent, but nothing like this had ever happened.

The only course open to Okonkwo was to flee from the clan. It was a crime against the earth goddess to kill a clansman, and a man who committed it must flee from the land. The crime was of two kinds, male and female. Okonkwo had committed the female, because it had been inadvertent. He could return to the clan after seven years.

That night he collected his most valuable belongings into head-loads. His wives wept bitterly and their children wept with them without knowing why. Obierika and half a dozen other friends came to help and to console him. They each made nine or ten trips carrying Okonkwo's yams to store in Obierika's barn. And before the cock crowed Okonkwo and his family were fleeing to his motherland. It was a little village called Mbanta, just beyond the borders of Mbaino.

As soon as the day broke, a large crowd of men from Ezeudu's quarter stormed Okonkwo's compound, dressed in garbs of war. They set fire to his houses, demolished his red walls, killed his animals, and destroyed his barn. It was the justice of the earth goddess, and they were merely her messengers. They had no hatred in their hearts against Okonkwo. His greatest friend, Obierika, was among them. They were merely cleansing the land which Okonkwo had polluted with the blood of a clansman.

Obierika was a man who thought about things. When the will of the goddess had been done, he sat down in his *obi* and mourned his friend's calamity. Why should a man suffer so grievously for an offence he had committed inadvertently? But although he thought for a long time he found no answer. He was merely led into greater complexities. He remembered his wife's twin children, whom he had thrown away. What crime had they committed? The earth had decreed that they were an offence on the land and must be destroyed. And if the clan did not exact punishment for an offence against the great goddess, her wrath was loosed on all the land and not just on the offender. As the elders said, if one finger brought oil it soiled the others.

The Country Bumpkin and the City Slickers

ALHAJI ABUBAKAR IMAM

This is a modern story based upon old traditions; it appears in *Magana Jari Ce,* Vol. I, by Alhaji Abubakar Imam, in the Hausa language of Nigeria.

Some young men from the city were once sitting about by the roadside when a yokel came past leading a donkey which he was going to sell in the market. Ahead of him there happened to be a country dancer and a drummer who were also on their way to the market where they were going to put on a show. The drummer was drumming, the dancer was going through his antics, throwing up a hoe and catching it again, and the yokel was following along behind with his mouth open and his eyes popping out of his head.

When the young men at the roadside saw that the yokel was paying no attention to his donkey one of them said: 'Don't look now but I'm going to take the donkey off that clot without his knowing it.'

'You're joking' said his friends. 'It's not dark, so you can't steal it, and you can't take it by force.'

The young man jumped up and followed the yokel, however, and the others tagged along behind. When he had got close enough he undid the rope round the donkey's neck and tied it round his arm. Then he turned the donkey over to his friends who drove it away. All this time the pull on the rope had never slackened and so the yokel, his mouth still open, had gone marching happily along, watching the dancer.

As soon as the young man saw that his friends had got safely away with the donkey, he dug in his heels and stopped. Even then the yokel did not turn round, because he was afraid of missing something that the dancer might do, and all he did was pull and coax and coax and pull. At last, however, when he realized that the donkey was not following, he turned round to give it a clout and came face to face not with the donkey but with the young man.

'Hey' he cried in surprise 'what's going on here?'

'It's a strange story' said the young man 'and you must stop and hear it. I'm your donkey' he went on 'but I haven't always been a donkey. Before that I was a man like yourself and I used to live with my mother. Then one day my youthful folly led me astray and I drank some beer. When I got home my mother said something about it—it was nothing to get excited about really but you know how it is when a man has taken drink—he doesn't realize what he's doing. Anyway, I swore at her. She looked at me and said: "Is it me you're swearing at? Have we come to this, then, that children now go about abusing their parents?" You must remember of course that she was a witch. "Yes" I said "I did swear at you. And who d'you think you are, anyway, if people can't swear at you?" At this she put up her hands and prayed that I should be turned into a donkey. And from that day to this a donkey is what I've been. That's how I came into your hands. But now that I've changed back to being a man again I know that she must have forgiven me.'

When the yokel heard all this he was very moved.

'For God's sake' he said 'do as your parents tell you. You're a fine-looking young man but you've been spoilt. You mustn't let the lure of youth lead you astray again.'

The young man listened to this sermon like a penitent.

'Very well' he said when the yokel had done. 'I'll follow your advice. . . .'

When he got home, the yokel told his wife everything that had happened and they reproached themselves for all the indignities which they had put upon the young man when they had thought him to be a donkey.

Now three days later there was another market and the young men put the yokel's donkey up for sale. As it happened, the yokel had originally meant to sell his Jack and buy a Jenny and so now he went to the market again to look for what he wanted. There he saw and recognized his old donkey.

'Shame on you!' he said, addressing himself to the donkey. 'You've paid no attention to anything I told you. That's always the way with you drunkards—you go your own way and let down people who try to help you. . . . Well, you'll have to get yourself out of the mess this time—I wash my hands of you.'

So saying he gave the donkey a kick and went his way. . . .

Beyond Those Hills

HENRY OLELA

AND

MARY JANE NEUENDORFFER

Henry Olela, a native of Mbita on Homa Bay in Lake Victoria, Kenya, graduated from Hiram College and Western Reserve in Ohio, and he holds the Ph.D. degree from Florida State University. His collaborator, Mrs. Neuendorffer, is with the Institute for Service Education for the African Primary School Science Development. *Beyond Those Hills* (1966) is a first novel, and is an official text in the Kenya schools. Olela has had a second novel accepted for publication. This is an excerpt from Chapter 2 of *Beyond Those Hills*.

Father, Okech, and Juma worked silently up and down the rows of growing millet. Once, Okech called out to Juma, 'You were a clever one, wanting to go fishing to escape the weeding.'

Juma had often wondered what it would be like to farm in another climate. Here in the Lowlands, if weeds were not pulled up every day they threatened to take over the gardens. Father was a man who took pride in a good crop. He not only made a thorough job of such routine chores as weeding, but also put to use all the modern methods he knew to improve the yield from the land.

In the matter of farming, Juma's father had become a leader in the area. Others came for his decisions on the best time to plough, to plant, and to harvest. Year after year, he never tired of the same routines over and over again. Walking through the gardens in February, crumbling the earth to test it, planting and watching the first seedlings appear, always brought a contented expression to Father's usually stern face. 'Land is life,' he said. 'With land, a man can feed his family; without it, a man is nothing.'

Juma wished that his father thought as highly of education.

An hour passed. The air, heavy with moisture, grew ominously still. Father leaned on his hoe, wiped the sweat from his brow, and gazed at the darkening sky. 'We'll have to stop and take cover soon,' he called to his sons. He pointed to a heavy cloud moving rapidly over the lake.

The cloud grew denser, the sky blacker, and Juma's heart was filled with anxiety for Grandfather, out in the canoe, with only Uncle Owino to help him haul the nets.

'Juma, run down to the beach and watch for *Situma*,' his father told him. 'Okech and I will work until the storm breaks.'

Juma was quick to leap over the rows of millet, place his hoe with the pile of tools, and dash away. He raced through other gardens, hopping over and around the growing young plants; he ran past the grazing areas where animals raised their heads to stare nervously after him. When he neared his own home, the sound of his grandmother's singing as she ground the day's millet came sweetly to his ear. Her melody ceased abruptly when the sun was covered by the storm cloud, turning day into a false twilight.

Flashing by his gate, Juma called out reassuringly to her. 'I'm going to help Grandfather unload the catch.' Although he tried to reassure his grandmother, Juma did not feel confident of *Situma's* return. Grandfather could not yet have hauled in all his nets, and being a stubborn man, as well as a courageous one, he would probably brave the storm until the full catch had been taken aboard.

On the path to the lake, he heard the splash of oars and men's voices. Breathlessly, he burst onto the beach. *Situma* was not among the incoming canoes. Anxiously, he asked each fisherman, 'Have you seen *Situma?*'

Each man shook his head.

Juma sighted one more craft. His heart lifted, until he saw it was not *Situma* but *Wanane*. He called to the owner, 'Have you seen my grandfather and uncle?'

The man pointed out toward the fishing grounds. 'The last I saw of *Situma*, a full net was being hauled aboard.'

A whistling wind eddied the angry-grey water. Sky and lake became so black, it seemed that night had returned.

The last fisherman to leave the beach shouted against the wind, 'Take cover, Juma. This will be a bad one.'

'I'll wait for *Situma*,' he shouted in reply.

At that instant, sky and lake blended in a wall of water. Torrential rain descended. Lightning flashed in zigzag patterns across the sky. Thunder rolled, echoing from the mainland hills. Juma ran to crouch beneath an overturned canoe on the beach. There he waited while the brief but violent storm spent its fury.

When the downpour subsided, Juma wriggled from beneath the canoe. He splashed through pools of foaming water and rushed back to the edge of the sand where angry waves still slapped the shore.

He peered across the lake, scanning the horizon for any sign of a canoe. Nothing moved but the water. Disheartened, he turned from the beauty of the azure sky, now sparkling clear after the storm.

Juma's downcast air brought encouraging words from Father when they met on the path. 'Your grandfather probably took shelter somewhere else,' he said, but his face did not reflect the heartiness of his voice.

The owner of the canoe *Wanane* returned to the beach and hailed them. 'I'll take you out to make a search,' he offered.

'Please, let me come along,' Juma begged.

Father gave his consent. Juma pushed *Wanane* from the sand, sprang through the shallows, and hopped lightly aboard to join the men. At Father's suggestion, *Wanane's* owner headed directly for the fishing grounds.

Juma looked towards the shore. He saw Grandmother's tiny figure standing there. The very way she stood showed her concern. Aunt Adhiambo, Uncle Owino's wife, came up beside her. The low murmur of mourning, begun by the women, was abruptly hushed when men appeared in their midst. A second canoe was launched to help in the search.

The distance grew between *Wanane* and the shore until the figures on the beach became only shifting dots to Juma's eyes. He settled down to the task of searching the horizon. The turmoil of waves had not subsided, and sighting anything took a sharp eye. Juma glanced often at his father. When Father shifted his gaze, Juma checked the same expanse of water. In this way they thoroughly covered a wide area. Once, Father's worried frown was replaced with a smile for Juma as if to tell him, 'We work well together.'

They both spotted the bobbing object at the same time. It was *Situma*, capsized but still afloat, with nets caught on the sides and streaming like broken wings on the water. They drew alongside, and found no sign of life.

Father's wail of sorrow rent the air.

He shook off his momentary grief. 'We must circle the area,' he said. 'Leave *Situma* to the waves; they will carry it ashore.'

Wanane moved off. The second canoe from Lutare Beach drew alongside. The men talked briefly, making a decision about further search.

'If we find nothing within half an hour, we will head for Kikolo Cove,' Father shouted after the second canoe. 'Perhaps they were rescued and taken there.'

The men gave a sign that they heard and understood.

Juma tried to believe in what even Father must know was small hope.

Juma fought back the sobs that rose in his aching throat. 'O, Grandfather!' he moaned. He wanted to jump into the water, swim to some far-off shore where Grandfather would surely be waiting for him. They would make a journey together; they would see everything in the world; all the wonders that Grandfather knew and shared with Juma in stories; the stories that had inspired Juma's longing to see those wonders for himself. He cried silently to the beloved elder, 'We'll go—we will—we'll see the world together.' And in Juma's mind, dazed with shock, he saw Grandfather's noble face, smiling his beautiful smile. Juma rose up as though to leap from the canoe.

Father caught his arm and sat him down. He clapped his hands before Juma's face. Juma came back to reality.

'Come now, take heart,' Father said. 'We may yet find your grandfather and uncle alive.'

In a short time, *Wanane* came upon Grandfather's body. A shout from the other canoe gave word that Uncle's body had also been sighted.

With tears streaming down their cheeks, Father and Juma lashed the lifeless form to *Wanane's* side. Juma felt pain that Grandfather could not be brought into the canoe, but knew the body should not be exposed too long to the air and blazing sun.

Juma bailed water from the canoe while *Wanane's* owner and Father paddled toward the island. *Wanane,* followed by the craft bearing Uncle's body, headed for the nearest point, Kikolo Cove.

There was no doubt that Grandmother and Aunt had kept watch. They would know from the movement of the canoes that a tragedy had occurred. Juma pictured the stream of men, women and children hurrying along the roadway from Lutare Beach to meet the incoming canoes.

At Kikolo Cove, many hands helped in the cutting of poles and the making of two litters. The bodies were placed on the litters, and water was poured over them as they were carried home.

In mournful procession, the people followed. Grandmother's low moans saddened Juma's heart. If Aunt or another woman wailed loudly, Grandmother raised her hand in a command for quiet. While it was but a short time until midday, she proudly followed the old custom that one must wait for the sun to reach the highest point before openly mourning a loss.

Grandfather and Uncle were laid within their own houses, and the doors were opened wide. At last, Grandmother's wails were heard, and the sound of her grief came from the open doorway and into every corner of the compound.

It was custom, made necessary by the climate, that burial take place before the day was over. Word of the evening funeral was sent out across the island.

Father asked Juma's best friend, Okinyi, to bicycle the eight miles to Mbita and find Juma's mother and sisters at the shops. Juma was concerned for the girls, and the deep sorrow he knew they would feel. His fifteen year old sister, Atieno, would be especially upset. She was a highly emotional girl and, as the first born granddaughter, she had always been dear to Grandfather's heart.

Juma told his friend that he hoped the women could be found before they heard of the tragic accident from someone else.

'I'll ride harder than I've ever done in my life,' Okinyi promised. 'When I do find your mother, I'll tell them only that the canoe is lost, then tell them the worst as gently as I can.'

Juma thanked him warmly, and Okinyi pedalled off.

By late afternoon, the home, indeed the whole village of Kamasengere was thronged with men and women from all parts of the island.

Grandfather had been a *Jaduong-gweng,* a group elder, who was held in respect by people of all positions. Juma was proud when the Chief of Rusinga Island arrived from Mbita Centre not long after Mother and the girls.

Sounds of mourning continued throughout the day. Men and women alike wailed for the loss of Grandfather and Uncle Owino. Drums beat out the rhythms of sorrow, trumpets and bugles blared in funeral dirges, and voices were raised in songs of grief.

Soon after dusk, Grandfather and Uncle were laid to rest in graves freshly dug near their own door-steps.

Grandmother and Aunt Adhiambo were spent with exhaustion and sorrow. Juma's mother stayed with Grandmother, and Atieno and Anyango went to Aunt's house to help care for her small children. Mourners who had come from a distance were housed in other homes in the village.

Juma shared Uncle Okomo's house with the Chief of Rusinga Island. The Chief had chosen to remain in the village until the next evening's ceremonies when Grandfather would be honoured by songs of tribute and praise.

Lugunga and Ouma, two well-known and accomplished guitarists of the island, arrived the next afternoon. Both men had prepared tributes for Grandfather and Uncle Owino.

Lugunga began. He had chosen the melody of an ancient canoe song which Grandfather himself had sung many times. Since the days of Juma's first trips in *Situma,* he had liked to listen to the rhythm of the oar hitting the water, and the beat of the song that told of the journeys of canoemen of old. Grandfather had sung:

> of the long hours the men paddled across the expanse of Lake Victoria . . .
> of the beautiful and mysterious fishes beneath the water . . .
> of the storms met and battled on the lake . . .
> and of the pleasures found when the canoemen arrived home once more . . .

Today, Lugunga made his song tell of Grandfather's journey through life:

> of his long years as an elder, leading and advising the clan . . .
> of the beautiful and sometimes mysterious happenings that were seen and understood by him . . .

of the storms met and battled by the people in his lifetime . . . and
the sorrows of famine, disease, and tribal quarrelling . . . and of
the death they brought to the young and old alike . . .
of the courage of Grandfather, who in times of famine on the island
walked to Awendo seventy miles distant on the mainland . . .
Awendo, where Rusinga folk had settled . . . Awendo, where if times
were good, the Rusinga folk would share their crops so the elder
might bring food to those in want on the island . . .
of pleasures found in happier days . . . when his sons and daughters
were married . . . when grandsons and granddaughters were
born . . . when the lake was bountiful with fish, and the gardens
were rich with harvest . . . when stomachs were full, and Kamasengere, Kaswanga, Wanyama, Waware, all Rusinga Island knew times
of plenty.

The good years and the bad years that Grandfather had known were
all recalled in song for the mourners. And they sang in reply—of this
or of that time when the elder had given wise counsel to each person.

Grandmother stood swaying to the rhythm of the guitarists' music.
She clapped her hands as the singers told of moments in her husband's
life that had been especially dear to her. She smiled at words of humour. Her sorrowful laughter rang out at the well-remembered story
of her husband as a young man when he had strived determinedly for
months to tame, and break to the plough, the wildest bull on the island. The words he said when the task was done: 'If I can tame a high-
spirited wife, of course I can tame a wild bull.'

After Juma had listened to the first tribute to Uncle Owino, he
slipped quietly away to a small rise behind Grandfather's house. There
he stood and gazed toward the lake and the distant hills on the farther
shore.

Juma watched the Sakwa Hills turn pink and purple with the fad-
ing sunset, dark blue with the gathering evening. He would never forget his grandfather, nor the elder's teachings and kindly advice.

Grandfather had said: 'Be patient. Work hard.'

'If only I could be as wise as he was,' Juma thought, and he made himself a promise to try.

He was too tired and too sad to think more deeply about the great
changes in family life which must occur now that the elder was gone.

Juma's eyes filled with tears, while in his heart he bade Grandfather a last farewell.

The Fig Tree

J. T. NGUGI

J. T. Ngugi of Kenya is a member of the Kikuyu tribe; he studied at Alliance High School and was introduced there to the works of Robert Louis Stevenson and Edgar Wallace. He read for an English degree at Makerere University College. He has published many short stories in African magazines and he has written several novels, including *Weep Not Child* (1964) and *A Grain of Wheat* (1967).

Mukami stood at the door; slowly and sorrowfully she turned her head and looked at the hearth. A momentary hesitation! The smouldering fire and the small stool by the fireside seemed to be calling her back. No! She had made up her mind. She must go! With a smooth, oiled upper-garment pulled tightly over her otherwise bare head, and then falling over her slim and youthful shoulders, she plunged into the lone and savage darkness—eerie yet still.

All was quiet and a sort of magic pervaded the air. Yet she felt it threatening. She felt overcome and overawed by the immensity of the darkness—unseeing, unfeeling, dead—that enveloped her. Quickly, she moved across the courtyard that she knew so well, fearing to make the slightest sound. Not a sound; all was dead. The courtyard, the four huts that belonged to her *airu* (co-wives), the silhouette of her man's hut and even her own, seemed to have joined together in one eternal chorus of mute condemnation of her action.

'You are leaving your man! Come back!' They all pleaded in their 'dead' silence of contempt yet pity. Defiantly, she crossed the courtyard and took the path that led down to the left gate. Slowly she opened the gate and then shut it. She stood a moment, and in that second Mukami realized that with the shutting of the gate, she had shut off a part of her existence. There would be no return. Tears were imminent as, with a heavy heart, she turned her back on her rightful place and began to move.

But where was she going? She did not know and she did not very much care. All she wanted was to escape and go! Go! go anywhere—

Masailand or Ukambani. She wanted to get away from the hearth, the courtyard, the huts, and the people—in a word, everything that reminded her of Muhoroini ridge and all its inhabitants. She would go and never return to him, her husb—. No! not her husband, but the man who wanted to kill her, who would have crushed her soul. He could no longer be her husband though he was the very same man she had adored so much. How she loathed him—but did she?

Thoughts of him came into her head like a mighty flood. Her young married life came back to her—Muthoga, Muthoga, her husband—a self-made man with four wives but with a reputation for harsh treatment of his wives; her father's reluctance to trust her into his hands and her dogged refusal to hearken to his remonstrance. For Muthoga had completely cast a spell on her. She wanted him, longed to join the retinue of his wives and children. Indeed, since her initiation, she had secretly but resolutely admired this man—his gait, dancing movements, and above all his bass voice and athletic figure. Everything around him smacked of mystery and power. And the courting had been short and strange. She could still remember the throbbing of her heart, his broad smile, and her hesitant acceptance of a string of oyster shells as a marriage token. This was followed by beer-drinking and the customary bride-price.

But people could not believe it and many young warriors whose offers she had scornfully brushed aside looked at her with scorn and resentment. 'Ah! Such youth and beauty to be sacrificed to an old man.' Many a man believed and in whispers declared that she had been bewitched. Indeed, she was—her whole heart had gone to this man!

No less memorable and sensational to her was the day they had carried her to this man's hut—a new hut that had been specially put up for her. She was going to the *shamba* when, to her surprise, three men approached her, apparently from nowhere. Then she knew! They were coming for her. She ought to have known, to have prepared herself for this! Her wedding day had come. Unceremoniously they swept her off the ground and for a moment she was really afraid and was putting up a real struggle to free herself from the firm yet gentle hands of the three men who were carrying her shoulder high. And the men! the men! They completely ignored her frenzied struggles. One of them had the cheek to pinch her, 'just to keep her quiet', as he carelessly remarked to one of his companions. The pinch shocked her in a very strange manner, a very pleasant strange manner. She ceased struggling and for the first time she noticed she was riding shoulder high on top of the soft seed-filled millet fingers which stroked her feet and sides as the men carried her. She felt really happy, but suddenly realized that she must keen all the way to her husband's home, must continue keening for a whole week.

The first season, wonderful! All his love and attention lavished on her. And, as in her youth, she became a target of jealousy and resentment from the other wives. A strong opposition grew. Oh women! Why could they not allow her to enjoy what they had enjoyed for years—his love? She could still recall how one of them, the eldest, had been beaten for refusing to get fire for Mukami from her hut. This ended the battle of words and deeds. It was now a mute battle. Mukami hardened towards them. She did not mind their insolence and ostracizing in which they had managed to enlist the sympathy of the whole village. But why should she mind? Had not the fulfillment of her dream, ambition, life and all, been realized in this man? She adored him, loved him, and fully gave herself to him—body, soul, and all. After all, what is life? Is it not giving and receiving?

Two seasons, three seasons, and the world she knew began to change. She had no child!

> A *thata*! A barren woman!
> No child to seal the bond between him and her.
> No child to dote on, hug and scold!
> No child to perpetuate the gone spirits of her man's ancestors and her father's blood.

O! She was defeated. She knew it. The others knew it. They whispered and smiled! Oh, how their oblique smiles of mute insolence and pride pierced her! But she had nothing to fear. Let them be victorious. She had still got her man.

Alas poor woman! So this was your hope? And without warning the man began to change and in time completely shunned her company and hut, confining himself more to his *thingira*. She felt embittered and sought him with her soul and body. Her heart bled for him yet found him not. Muthoga, the warrior, the farmer, the dancer had recovered his old hard-heartedness which had been temporarily subdued by her, and he began to beat her. He had found her quarrelling with the eldest wife, and all his accumulated fury, resentment, and frustration seemed to find an outlet as he beat her. Oh! the beating; the crowd that watched and never helped! But that was a preamble to such torture and misery that it culminated almost in her death that very morning.

He had called on her early and without a warning or explanation beat her so much that he left her for dead. She had not screamed—she had accepted her lot. And as she lay on the ground thinking it was now the end, it dawned on her that perhaps the others had been suffering as much because of her. Yes! She could see them being beaten and crying for mercy. But she resolutely refused to let such beating and hallucinations subdue her soul. She must conquer; and with that realization she had quickly made up her mind. This was no place for her, neither could she return to her place of birth to face her dear old considerate father again. She could not bear the shame.

The cold night breeze brought her back to her present condition. Tears, long suppressed, flowed down her cheeks as she hurried down the path that wound through the bush, down the valley and through the forest. It was so dark that she could hardly pick her way through the labyrinth of thorn and bush. The murmuring stream, the quiet bush and trees that surrounded her—did these sympathize with her or did they join with the kraal in silent denouncement of her action? But could they understand the frailties of men?

She followed the stream, and then crossed it at its lowest point where there were two or three stones on which she could step. She was still too embittered, too grieved to notice her surroundings. Her thoughts and speculations did not let her realize her grave danger! For was this not the place where the dead were thrown? Where the spirits of the dead hovered through the air, intermingling with trees, molesting strangers and intruders? She was angry with the world, her husband, but above all, with herself. Could she have been in the wrong all the time? Was this the price she must pay for her selfish grabbing of all the man's soul? But she had also sacrified her own soul, youth, and beauty for his sake. More tears and anguish of soul.

Oh spirits of the dead, come for me!
   Oh Murungu, god of Gikuyu and Mumbi,
      Who dwells on high Kerinyaga, yet is everything,
Why don't you release me from misery?
   Dear Mother Earth, why don't you open and swallow me up
      Even as you had swallowed Gumba—the Gumba who disappeared
         under Mikongoe roots?

She invoked the spirits of the living and the dead to come and carry her off, never to be seen again.

All of a sudden as if in answer to her invocations she heard a distant, mournful sound, pathetic yet real. The wind began to blow wildly and the last star that had so strangely comforted her, vanished. She was all alone in the gloom of the forest! Something cold and lifeless touched her. She jumped and at last did what the beating could not make her do—scream! The whole forest echoed with her scream. Naked fear now gripped her whole being and she shook all over—even her soul. And she realized she was not alone. Here and there, she saw a thousand eyes that glowed intermittently without any order all along the stream, while, to and fro, she felt herself being pushed by many invisible hands. The sight and the sudden realization that she was in the land of ghosts, alone, and far from home left her stone dead. She could not feel, think, or cry! It was fate—the will of *Murungu*. Lower and lower she sank onto the ground as the last traces of strength ebbed from her body. This was the end, the culmination of her dream and ambition. But it was all unreal. She did not really want to die. Life was sweet. She only wanted a chance to start life anew—a life of giving and not only of receiving.

Her misery was not at an end, for even as she lay on the ground, and even as the owl and hyena cried in the distance, the wind blew harder, the mournful sound grew louder and nearer—and it began to rain! Thunder! Lighting! The earth looked as if it would crack and open beneath her. But even as the lightning came and thunder struck she espied a tree in the distance—a huge tree it was, with the bush growing gently but reverently, bowing all around the trunk. And she knew— she knew, even as if the spirits had told her that this was THE TREE— the sacred Fig Tree, that is called *Mukuyu*—the altar of the all-seeing *Murungu*. 'Good lighting—you have revealed this to me. Here at last is a place of sanctuary.'

And thither she ran, defying the rain, the thunder, and even the 'Ghosts'. Her husband and all the people of Muhoroini ridge vanished into insignificance. All the load that had weighed upon her heart seemed to be lifted as she wearily ran through the thorny bush, knocking against the trees falling and waking. Her impotence was gone. Her worries were gone. Her one object was to reach the Fig Tree. It was a matter of life and death—a battle for life. There under the sacred Fig Tree, she would find sanctuary and peace. There, Mukami, would meet her God, *Murungu*, the God of her tribe.

The rain fell in torrents and the lightning became sharper and more frightening. But she would conquer. She must win. Her old defiance and determination had come back.

> Not rain, not thunder, not lighting.
> But *wee,* Oh creator.

So she ran despite her physical weakness. And she could feel her soul burning, a pleasant burning that made her womb dance. Now she was near the place of sanctuary—the altar of the Most High, the place of salvation. So towards the altar she ran—No, not running but flying, at least her soul must have been flying. For she felt as light as a feather. O little bird! She had wings! wings! wings. At last she reached there panting and breathless.

Far in the distance, the owl screamed! The piercing lightning came and threatened, and the thunder struck with a might that shook the earth. But she did not hear. She had lain asleep under the protecting arms of God's tree. The spell was on her again.

Mukami woke up with a start. What! Nobody? Surely that had been Mumbi, who standing beside her husband Gikuyu, had touched her—a gentle touch that went right through her body. No she must have been dreaming. What a strange beautiful dream. And Mumbi had said, I am the mother of the tribe. . . . She looked round. Darkness still. And there was the ancient tree, strong, unageing. How many secrets must you have told!

'I must go home! Go back to my husband and my tribe.' It was a new Mukami humble yet full of hope who said this. Then she fell asleep again. The spell. . . .

The sun was rising in the east and the rich yellowish streaks of light diffused through the forest to where Mukami was sitting, leaning against the tree. And as the straying streaks of light touched her skin, she felt a tickling sensation that went right through her body. Blood thawed in her veins and oh! she felt warm—so very warm, happy, and light. Her soul danced and her womb answered. And she she knew—knew that she was pregnant, had been pregnant for some time!!!

As Mukami stood up ready to go, she stared with unseeing eyes into space, while tears of deep gratitude and humility trickled down. Her eyes went beyond the forest, beyond the stream as if they were seeing something, something hidden in the distant future. And she saw the people of Muhoroini, her *airu* and her man—strong, unageing—standing amongst them. That was her rightful place, there beside her husband amongst the other wives. They must unite and support the tribe, giving it new life. Was Mumbi watching?

Far in the distance a cow lowed. Mukami stirred from her reverie!

'I must go!' She began to move. And the Fig Tree—huge, mysterious unperturbed—still stood and watched, sending forth a rich sympathizing warmth. . . .

Black African Poetry

Like all poetry, this is heightened expression of an experience conveying an attitude, an emotion, the shape of an identity. Much of the poetry of Africa is in the oral tradition, originally passed along from father to son, from mother to daughter, and only very recently written down. Some of the poetry is by contemporaries who are using a second language to express themselves. Translated into English the expression loses much of its original flavor, but there remains even in translation more than a hint of the passion of emotion, the strong rhythm characteristic of black Africans, and an unusual juxtaposition of words which is remarkably effective.

ORAL TRADITIONAL

Paddling Song

My dugout canoe goes
Swiftly down the river.

In every tree the monkeys
Are chattering and crying.
Oh, big jungle hunter,
Tell me of their trouble.

The little monkey broke his leg,
So they all are crying.

Then bend to your paddle,
Hunter of the river,
And tell the mother that
Her monkey-baby's crying:
The little monkey broke his leg.
They are all crying.

MAX EXNER
(Bantu Congo)

NIGERIA

Once Upon a Time

Once upon a time, son
they used to laugh with their hearts
and laugh with their eyes;
but now they only laugh with their teeth,
while their ice-block-cold eyes
search behind my shadow.

There was a time indeed
they used to shake hands with their hearts;
but that's gone, son.
Now they shake hands without hearts
while their left hands search
my empty pockets.

"Feel at home," "Come again,"
they say, and when I come
again and feel

at home, once, twice,
there will be no thrice—
for then I find doors shut on me.

So I have learned many things, son.
I have learned to wear many faces
like dresses—homeface,
officeface, streetface, hostface, cock-
tailface, with all their conforming smiles
like a fixed portrait smile.

And I have learned too
to laugh with only my teeth
and shake hands without my heart.
I have also learned to say, "Goodbye,"
when I mean "goodriddance";
to say "Glad to meet you,"
without being glad; and to say "It's been
nice talking to you," after being bored.

But believe me, son.
I want to be what I used to be
when I was like you. I want
to unlearn all these muting things.
Most of all, I want to relearn
how to laugh, for my laugh in the mirror
shows only my teeth like a snake's bare fangs!

So show me, son,
how to laugh; show me how
I used to laugh and smile
Once upon a time when I was like you.

GABRIEL OKARA

One Wife for One Man

Italicized line-by-line translation from West African pidgin-English by Francis Ernest
Kobina Parkes

I done try go to church, I done go for court.
I've tried the altar, I've tried the court-room.
Dem all dey talk about di *new culture*
All both of them talk about is this "new culture."
Dem talk about *equality*, dem mention *divorce*.
They talk about "equality" and proclaim "divorce."
Dem holler am so-tay my ear nearly cut;
They shout it so much my ear-drums nearly burst;
One wife for one man.

My fader before my fader get him wife barku
My father's father had plenty of wives.
E no' get equality palaver; he live well
He did all right without all this "equality" humbug.
For he be oga for im own house.
And he was the boss in his own house.
Bot dat time done pass before white man come wit im
But since then the white man's come with this stuff about
One wife for one man.

Tell me how una woman no go make *yonga*
Tell me how a man can keep a woman from being bossy
Wen'e know say na'im only dey
When she knows well she has no lawful rival.
Suppose say-make God no 'gree-'e no born at all.
Suppose it is God's will she has no offspring at all.
A' tell you dat man bind dey craze wey start
I tell you the man must've been crazy who suggested
One wife for one man.

Jus' tell me how one wife fir do one man?
Just tell me how one wife can be enough for a man?
How man go fit stay all time for him house,
What can make a man stay home all the time
For when belle done kommotu.
When his one wife is pregnant as she can be?
How many pickin, self, one woman fir born
After all, how many children can one woman bear
When there's just one wife for one man?

Suppose self, say na so-so woman your wife dey born;
Suppose your wife's womb houses only females;
Suppose your wife sabe book, no' sabe make chop;
Suppose your wife is educated and doesn't know how to cook;
Den, how you go tell man make 'e no go out
Then how can you tell a man not to run around—
Sake of dis divorce: Bo, dis culture no waya o!
Or he'll be threatened by divorce. Man, this "new culture" is awful:
Just one wife for one man!

FRANK AIG-IMOUKHUEDE

Abiku

Abiku is the Yoruba myth of infant mortality, meaning literally, "born-to-die." It is
believed that the dead child returns to plague the mother.

In vain your bangles cast
Charmed circles at my feet.
I am Abiku, calling for the first
And repeated time.

Must I weep for goats and cowries,
For palm oil and the sprinkled ash?
Yams do not sprout in armlets
To earth Abiku's limbs.

So when the snail is burnt in his shell
With the heated fragment, brand me
Deeply on the breast. You must know him
When Abiku calls again.

I am the squirrel teeth, cracked.
The riddle of the palm. Remember
This and dig me deeper still into
The god's swollen foot.

Once and the repeated time
Ageless though I puke. And when

You pour libations, each finger
Points me near the way I came, where

The ground is wet with mourning,
White dew suckles flesh-birds,
Evening befriends the spider,
Trapping flies in wine-froth.

Night, and Abiku sucks the oil
From lamps. Mothers! I'll be the
Suppliant snake coiled on the doorstep,
Yours the killing cry.

The ripest fruit was saddest.
Where I crept, the warmth was cloying.
In the silence of webs Abiku moans
Shaping mounds from the yolk.

WOLE SOYINKA

ZAIRE

Dawn in the Heart of Africa

For a thousand years, you, African, suffered like a beast,
Your ashes strewn to the wind that roams the desert.
Your tyrants built the lustrous, magic temples
To preserve your soul, preserve your suffering.
Barbaric right of fist and the white right to a whip,
You had the right to die, you also could weep.
On your totem they carved endless hunger, endless bonds,
And even in the cover of the woods a ghastly cruel death
Was watching, snaky, crawling to you
Like branches from the holes and heads of trees
Embraced your body and your ailing soul.
Then they put a treacherous big viper on your chest:
On your neck they laid the yoke of fire-water,
They took your sweet wife for glitter of cheap pearls,

Your incredible riches that nobody could measure.
From your hut, the tom-toms sounded into dark of night
Carrying cruel laments up mighty black rivers
About abused girls, streams of tears and blood,
About ships that sailed to countries where the little man
Wallows in an anthill and where the dollar is king,
To that damned land which they called a motherland.
There your child, your wife were ground, day and night
In a frightful, merciless mill, crushing them in dreadful pain.
You are a man like others. They preach you to believe
That good white God will reconcile all men at last.
By fire you grieved and sang the moaning songs
Of a homeless beggar that sinks at strangers' doors.
And when a craze possessed you
And your blood boiled through the night
You danced, you moaned, obsessed by father's passion.

Like fury of a storm to lyrics of a manly tune
From a thousand years of misery a strength burst out of you
In metallic voice of jazz, in uncovered outcry
That thunders through the continent like gigantic surf.
The whole world surprised, wakes up in panic
To the violent rhythm of blood, to the violent rhythm of jazz,
The white man turning pallid over this new song
That carries torch of purple through the dark of night.
The dawn is here, my brother! Dawn! Look in our faces,
A new morning breaks in our old Africa.
Ours alone will now be the land, the water, mighty rivers
Poor African surrendered for a thousand years.
Hard torches of the sun will shine for us again
They'll dry the tears in eyes and spittle on your face.
The moment when you break the chains, the heavy fetters,
The evil, cruel times will go never to come again.
A free and gallant Congo will arise from black soil,
A free and gallant Congo—black bossom from black seed!

PATRICE EMERY LUMUMBA

Kenya

The Village

Kanyairi, Village of Toil,
Village of unending work.
Like a never drying spring,
Old women dark and bent
Trudge along with their hoes
To plots of weedy maize.
Young wives like donkeys
From cock crow to setting of the sun
Go about their timeless duties,
Their scraggy figures like bows set in a row,
Plod up and down the rolling village farms
With loads on their backs
And babies tied to their bellies.
In the fields all day they toil
Stirring up the soil with hands and knives
Like chickens looking for worms.
Nothing here seems to sit still.
Even the village church is like a favourite well
Where the "Revivalists" with their loudspeakers
Never cease calling people
To confess their sins and drink the Water of Life.
At dawn men ride away leaving the womenfolk
To fend for the bony goats and the crying children.

MARINA GASHE

FRANK ABIODUN AIG-IMOUKHUEDE, a graduate of the University College of Ibadan, was born near Ife in the Benin Province of Nigeria of Yoruba parentage. His father was a clergyman who translated the New Testament into a dialect of the Bini language. He wrote plays for student productions while at college and upon graduation was employed by the Broadcasting House in Lagos, and later as reporter for the *Daily Express*. He frequently writes in pidgin-English, which is the lingua-franca of West Africa.

MARINA GASHE and her husband, Elimo Njau, are teachers. Marina studied at Makerere College in Uganda. She is a member of the Kikuyu tribe from Kenya. She won the drama festival award with her first play entitled "The Scar." Her husband is a painter who comes from the slopes of Mt. Kilimanjaro. They now reside in Kampala, Kenya.

PATRICE EMERY LUMUMBA, reported to have been assassinated in February, 1961, by political opponents, was the first Premier of the Republic of the Congo and has gained a kind of immortality as a symbol of Pan-Africanism. He is the author of *Congo, My Country.*

GABRIEL IMOMOTIMI OBAINGAING OKARA is considered by many critics as one of the outstanding poets of Nigeria. He has traveled widely and given poetry readings in the United States, in Europe and in Africa. His work has been translated into several languages. He served as Press Agent for the Nigerian Information Service at Enugu.

WOLE SOYINKA was born in Abeokuta, Nigeria, in 1934, of Yoruba parentage. He graduated from Government College and Leeds University in England. At one time he was a writer for the Royal Court Theatre in London. His play "The Invention" was staged there. He has been Research Fellow at University College, Ibadan, where many of his plays were produced, among them "The Lion and the Jewel," "The Swamp Dwellers," and "Dance of the Forest." He has traveled in both the United States and in Australia to inspect the work of university theatres.

Conclusion

The artistic expression of Africa—exotic, diverse and complex—offers rich resources for further investigation. To draw any definitive conclusions from a rather cursory survey is like trying to analyze a handful of smoke.

Is there emerging a recognizable identity which may become clearly and distinctly typical of Africa or typically "negritude" in style? Is it possible that an interracial synthesis may supersede and surpass the purely African identity? Will a superficial modernity vaguely Western via current trends in mass production (plastics and the like, encouraging the shoddy and the cheap) level off artistic expression in contemporary Africa and breed mediocrity?

No man can predict these things with certainty, for the African as well as the Easterner and the Westerner lives with violence and revolution and rebellion, with scientific inventions potentially available literally to blow him up or to disintegrate and pulverize his existence and this planet! The hippies and the "psychedelic crowd" begin to pervade the universe—with their dead-pan faces and the vacancy of "hollow men"—the dropouts and the tranquilized receding inexorably to vegetable immobility. In the West, for instance, emerges the drama of the absurd, the advent of the "happening," "instant art" culminating now and again in its practitioners protesting against the Establishment by flinging aside all modesty and in public performance stripping down to the naked flesh! Or focusing upon violence and vile language. The coke bottle and the label on a can of soup become "Pop Art."

The condition in contemporary African art may be equally frenetic and evasive, but it is also fascinating and viable. Out of the submerged identity of the ancient African past, tempered by the cultures of foreign occupation, there may result an epoch of artistic excellence.

The centuries old method used in fashioning the Benin bronzes of Nigeria—the *cire perdue* or "lost wax process"—might symbolize what could occur.

The molded clay of the original image might represent the traditional basic pre-literate artistic source; the layers of wax applied on top of the clay might represent the super-imposition of foreign cultures; the firing might be the strife and the conflict and the purging which results in "losing the wax of exploitation"; the pouring on of the molten bronze might represent the influx and the insurgence of new talent and new skills which become the newly molded covering, the new identity which may be further shaped and refined and polished, quite possibly to become recognized as a truly significant and universally accepted artistic production.

Will the result be Negritude? An African identity? A Universal synthesis? Or a little of each?

In an interview, Ayo Ogunshaye, one of the Deans of University College in Ibadan, Nigeria, who is considered one of the most formidable of the new Africa's young intelligentsia, made these very considerable comments:

> . . . (*What values*), *distinctive African values, are not only as they say worth preserving . . . but also worth exporting?*

> I would say, first, the African's deeply historical conception of society as a unit made up of the ancestors, the living and future generations

—then his spiritual attitude to life and his attachment to communal life and communal responsibilities—finally, his sense of rhythm as manifested in his poetry, his music, and his sculpture. The trouble has been that the education of the African in modern times has been such as to make him not only ignorant of but sneakingly ashamed of his own cultural heritage. He has to be re-educated. Then he may be able to understand himself and his past and appreciate what is good in it.

. . . But would you subscribe to the notion that there is an inherent quality of "Africanness," something with which people are born because they are Africans?

No, this seems to me a racial myth, and a dangerous one at that. All human beings are what they are because of their environment, their history, their culture, their upbringing. The African is no exception. There is nothing peculiar in his blood (except, probably, a relative immunity to some tropical diseases). If he looks at life in a certain way, if he has certain conceptions of beauty and rhythm, it is because he has learned to do so. In this respect the African is at one with the rest of humanity. There are some distinctive African values, but I am convinced that the African shares with other peoples—who are at the same stage of development, or who live under similar geographical conditions—similar attitudes and problems.

. . . If I were to press you to write a prescription for your fellow Africans, how would it go?

Oh, I suppose it would go something like this: "Be yourselves, know your past and your culture, for a people without a sense of values is like a ship without a rudder. To your cultural heritage don't hesitate to add from other cultures some ideas and some techniques which you think will help you build a better world. In doing this you will only be returning the compliment of the Western world—which did not hesitate to draw on your art and music in order to revitalize its own. In the world of culture we are all builders, all borrowers and lenders. (1)

Building and borrowing and lending may be, indeed, a fundamental principle which has helped produce all cultures of lasting significance.

Man's finest artistic creations may be specifically African or Oriental or Western and at the same time universal in appeal. The study of the work of artists who have attained a measure of identity while "building and borrowing and lending" may support the contention that an interchange of cultures can unite nations and races and still permit each to retain some of the uniqueness of individual identity.

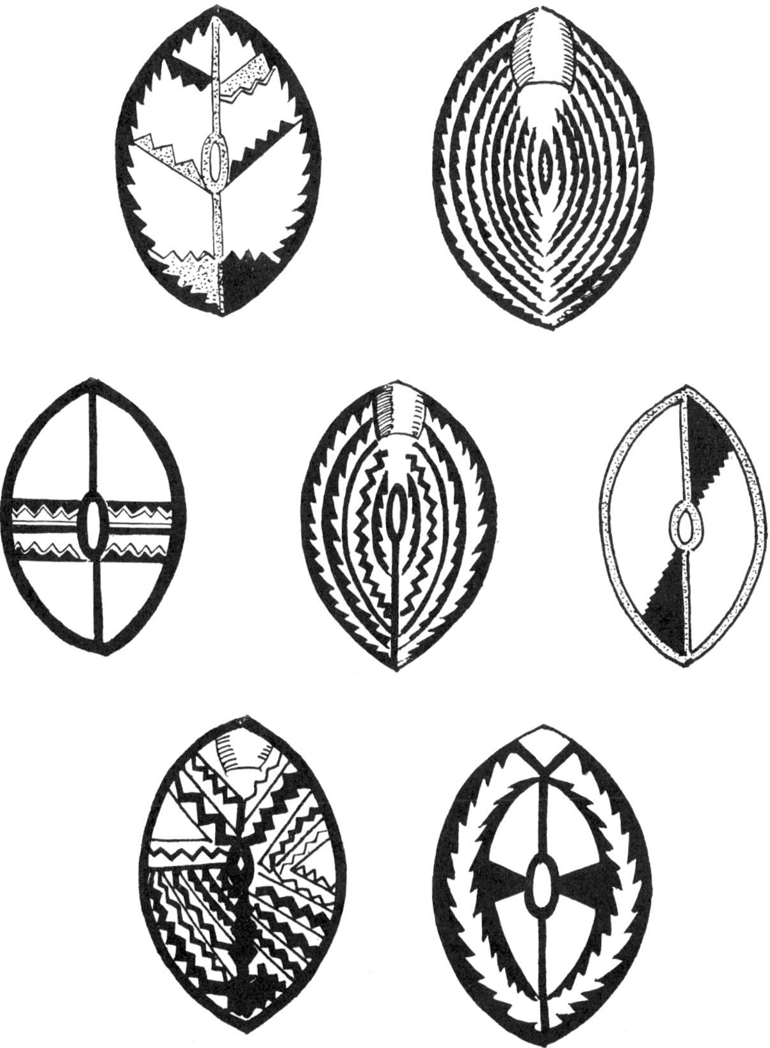

Fig. 34. Ornamental motifs on shields for ceremonial dances of Kikuyu youths. Kenya. Painted and stained leather. Varying sizes; some are the height of a man.

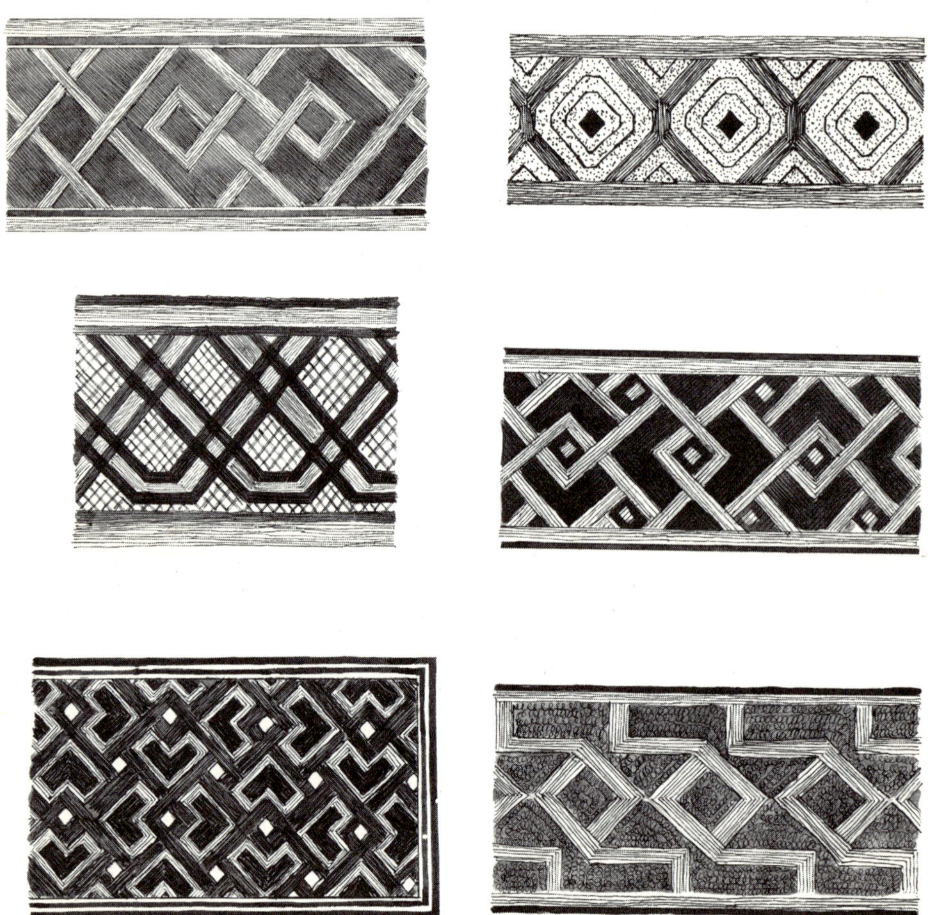

Fig. 35. Raffia/Fabric designs. Baluba, Zaire. Stained and/or woven raffia embroidery; many of these designs are adapted for contemporary fabrics.

References and Citations

INTRODUCTION:

1. Kenyatta, *Facing Mount Kenya,* pp. 309–310.
2. Basden, *Among the Ibos of Nigeria,* pp. 9–10.
3. Wingert, *Primitive Art,* p. 72.

GENERAL INFORMATION:

1. Wallbank, *Civilization Past and Present,* p. 542ff.
2. *Larousse Encyclopedia of Prehistoric & Ancient Arts,* p. 85.
3. *World Almanac,* 1967 estimates.
4. *Ibid.*
5. *Guide to the Democratic Republic of the Congo,* p. 8ff.
6. *Ibid.,* p. 16.
7. Duerden, *African Art,* p. 37.

TRADITIONAL ARTS:

1. Duerden, *op. cit.,* p. 12.
2. *Ibid.,* p 23.
3. *Ibid.,* p. 9.
4. *Ibid.,* p. 8.
5. *Ibid.,* p. 14.
6. Basden, *op. cit.,* pp. 185–190.
7. *Encyclopedia of World Art,* Vol. 2, p. 240.
8. Kenyatta, *op. cit.,* pp. 130–138.
9. *Guide to Congo,* p. 17ff.
10. Johnston, *A Selection of Hausa Stories,* Introd. ff.

COLONIAL ARTS:

1. *Encyclopedia of World Arts,* Vol. 2, p. 216ff.
2. *Ibid.,* Vol. 1, p. 47.
3. *Ibid.,* Vol. 10, p. 245.
4. *Ibid.,* Vol. 2, p. 231.
5. Duerden, *op. cit.,* p. 14.
6. Brown, *Contemporary African Art and Artists,* p. 52.
7. *Nigeria,* pub. of Nigerian Embassy, p. 11ff.
8. Brown, *op. cit.,* p. 56.
9. Basden, *op. cit.,* pp. 131–134.

CONTEMPORARY ARTS:

1. Brown, *op. cit.,* p. 64.
2. *Ibid.,* p. 65.
3. Beier, *Contemporary Art in Africa,* p. 110.
4. Brown, *op. cit.,* p. 56.
5. *Ibid.,* p. 58.
6. Beier, *op. cit.,* pp. 92–94.
7. *Ibid.,* p. 42.
8. Brown, *op. cit.,* p. 62.
9. *Ibid.,* p. 55.
10. *Larousse, op. cit.* p. 87.
11. Brown, *op. cit.,* p. 53.
12. *Ibid.,* p. 58.
13. *Encyclopedia of World Art,* Vol. 10, p. 245ff.
14. *Ibid.,* p. 249.
15. *Encyclopedia of World Art,* Vol. 1, p. 49.
16. *Guide to Congo,* p. 8ff.
17. *Ibid.,* p. 18.
18. *Ibid.,* p. 21.
19. Beier, *op. cit.,* p. 14.

CONCLUSION:

1. Lasky, *African for Beginners,* pp. 58–62.

Selective Bibliography

Books, Magazines, Pamphlets.

Abraham, W. E., *The Mind of Africa,* The University of Chicago Press, Chicago, 1962.

Abrash, Barbara, *Black African Literature in English since 1952* (Works and Criticism), Johnson Reprint Corp., New York 1967.

Achebe, Chinua, *Arrow of God,* International University Booksellers, New York, 1967.

Achebe, Chinua, *Things Fall Apart,* Heinemann, Ltd., London, 1958.

Adamson, Joy, *Born Free,* Pantheon Press, New York, 1960.

Adamson, Joy, *The Peoples of Kenya,* Harcourt, Brace & World Inc., New York, 1967.

African Encounter, A Selected Bibliography of Books, Films, and other Materials for Promoting Understanding of Africa Among Young Adults, American Library Association, Chicago, 1963.

African/English Literature: A Survey—Anthology of Prose and Poetry up to 1965, ed. Ann Tibble, International University Booksellers, New York, 1965.

African Myths and Tales, ed. Susan Feldman, Dell Publishing Compay, Inc., New York, 1970.

African New Writing, ed. Cullen Young, Lutterworth Press, London, 1947.

African Voices: An Anthology of Native African Writing, ed. Peggy Rutherfoord, The Vanguard Press, Inc., New York, 1958, 1960.

African Writing Today, ed. Ezekiel Mphahlele, Penguin-Books, Middlesex, England, 1967.

An African Treasury, ed. Langston Hughes, Crown Publishers, Inc., New York, 1960.

"Art and Mankind," *Larousse Encyclopedia of Byzantine and Medieval Art,* ed. Rene Huggbe, Prometheus Press, Inc., New York, 1958.

"Arts and Mankind," *Larousse Encyclopedia of Prehistoric and Ancient Art,* Prometheus Press, New York, 1958.

A Selected Bibliography of Traditional and Modern Africa, ed. Peter C. W. Gutkind and John B. Webster, Maxwell Graduate School, Syracuse University, Syracuse, N. Y., 1968.

A Selection of African Prose (Vol. I—Oral; Vol. II—Written), ed. W. H. Whiteley, initiated by UNESCO, The Clarenden Press, Oxford, 1964.

A Selection of Hausa Stories, compiled and translated by H. A. S. Johnston, The Clarenden Press, Oxford, 1966.

"Backgroud Notes"—Department of State Publication, Office of Media Services, Bureau of Public Affairs, Superintendent of Documents, U.S. Government Printing Office, Washington, D.C. 20412.

Basden, G. T., *Among the Ibos of Nigeria,* Barnes and Noble, Inc., New York, 1966.

Basden, G. T., *Niger Ibos,* Barnes and Noble, Inc., New York, 1966.

Beier, Ulli, *Art in Nigeria,* Cambridge University Press, 1960.

Beier, Ulli, *Contemporary Art in Africa,* Praeger, New York, 1968.

Bibliography of Doctoral Research on the Negro 1933–1966, compiled by Earle H. West, Howard University, Xerox Corp., Universal Micro-films, 1969.

Biggers, John, *Ananse,* University of Texas Press, 1962.

Brown, Evelyn, *African Contemporary Art and Artists,* The Harmon Foundation, New York, 196–.

Caesaire, A., *Return to my Native Land,* International University Booksellers, New York (Paris 1968).

Cartet, Wilfred, *Whispers from a Continent—The Literature of Contemporary Black Africa,* Random House, New York, 1969.

Catalogue of the African Collection, Moorland Foundation, Howard University, ed. Dorothy B. Porter, Howard University Press, Washington, D.C., 1958.

Chase, Ilka, *Elephants Arrive at Half-Past Five,* Doubleday and Company, Inc., New York, 1963.

Clark, John Pepper, *America, Their America,* International University Booksellers, New York, 1969.

Contemporary African Art, Studio Intenational, London and Africana Publishing Corporation, New York, 1970.

Continuity and Change in African Culture, ed. William R. Bascom and Melville J. Herskovitz, Phoenix Books, University of Chicago Press, 1959.

Courlander, Harold and Herzog, George, *The Cow-tail Switch and Other West African Stories,* Holt, New York, 1947.

Davidson, Basil, *Africa: History of a Continent,* The Macmillan Company, New York, 1963.

Davidson, Basil, *Africa in History,* The Macmillan Company, New York, 1968.

Dineson, Isak, *Out of Africa,* Random House, New York, 1952.

Dinesen, Isak, *Shadows on the Grass,* Random House, New York, 1961.

Duerden, Dennis, *African Art,* The Hamlyn Publishing Group, Ltd., Middlesex, England, 1968.

Edwards, P., *A Ballad Book for Africa,* International University Booksellers, New York (London 1968).

Ekwensi, Cyprian, *Jagua Nana,* Fawcett Premier Books, Greenwich, Connecticut, 1961.

Ekwensi, Cyprian, *People of the City,* Fawcett Premier Books, Greenwich, Connecticut, 1961.

Encyclopedia of World Art, Vols. 1, 2, 10—Articles on African Culture and Bantu Culture, pub. in English by McGraw-Hill, London, 1959.

Fagg, William, *Nigerian Images: The Splendor of African Sculpture,* Praeger Publishers, New York, 1963.

Gardner, Helen, *Art Through the Ages,* 4th edition, Harcourt Brace and World Inc., New York, 1959.

Gatanyu, J., *The Battlefield,* The International University Booksellers (Nairobi 1967).

Gide, Andre, *Travels in the Congo,* University of California Press, Los Angeles, 1962.

Guide to the Democratic Republic of the Congo, Publication of the Embassy of the Republic of the Congo, Washington, D.C., 1969.

Huggke, Rene, *Ideas and Images in the World of Art—Dialogue with the Visible,* Henry N. Abrams, Inc., New York, 1959.

The Handbook of Africa, ed. Violain I. Junod, New York University Press, New York, 1963.

Hausa and Fulani Proverbs, ed. C. E. J. Whitting, International University Booksellers (Lagos 1940, Farnborough, England, 1967) New York, 1969.

Introduction to African Literature, An Anthology of Critical Writing from "Black Orpheus," ed. Ulli Beier, Northwestern University Press, Evanston, Illinois, 1967.

Jahn, Janheinz, *Munti: An Outline of the New African Culture,* Grove Press, Inc., New York, 1961.

Janson, A. W., *History of Art—A Survey of the Major Visual Arts from the Dawn of History to the Present Day,* Prentice-Hall, Inc. & Henry N. Abrams., New York, 1962.

Kenyatta, Jomo, *Facing Mount Kenya—The Tribal Life of the Gikuyu* (Secker and Warburg, 1959), Vintage-Random House, New York, 1962.

Kibera, L. and S. Kahiaga, *Potent Ash: Short Stories* (Nairobi 1968), International University Booksellers, New York, 1969.

Laski, Melvin J., *Africa for Beginners,* J. B. Lippencott Co., Philadelphia and New York, 1962.

Laudeck, Beatrice, *Echoes of Africa in Folk Songs of the Americas,* Instrumental Arrangements by Milton Kays, McKay, New York, 1961.

Leiris, Michel, "The African Negroes and the Arts of Carving and Sculpture" in *Intercultural Relations—Their Contribution to International Understanding,* UNESCO, Paris, 1953.

Leuzinger, Elsy, Africa: *the Art of the Negro Peoples* (trans. by Ann E. Keep) in *Art of the World Series, Non-European Culture,* McGraw Hill, New York, 1960.

Litafi na Tatsuniyea na Hausa, ed. Frank Edgar, Belfast, 1913.

Lumumba, Patrice, *Congo, My Country,* Praeger, New York, 1962.

Mphahele, Ezekul, *The African Image,* Praeger, New York, 1962.

Modern Poetry from Africa, ed. Gerald Moore and Ulli Beier, Penguin Books, Middlesex, England, 1963.

New Approaches to African Literature, ed. J. A. Ramsaran, Ibadan Press, Ibadan, Nigeria, 1965.

Nigeria, publication of the Nigerian Embassy, Washington, D.C., 1969.

Ngugi, J., *A Grain of Wheat,* International University Booksellers, New York (London 1967).

Ngugi, J., *Weep Not Child* (New ed. with an introd. and notes by Ime Ikiddeh), International University Booksellers, New York (London 1967).

Ogot, Grace, *Land Without Thunder,* International University Booksellers, New York, 1969.

Ogot, Grace, *The Promised Land,* International University Booksellers, New York (Nairobi 1969).

Ojike, Mbonu, *My Africa,* John Day Inc., New York, 1946.

Olela, Henry and Mary Jane Neuendorffer, *Beyond Those Hills,* Evans Bros., Ltd., London, 1966.

Parrinder, Geoffrey, *African Mythology,* The Hamlyn Publishing Group, Middlesex, England, 1968.

Phase Two of the Beat Goes On: A Supplementary Guide to Resources for African Music and Dance, African Bibliographic Center (Current Reading List Series, Vol. 7, No. 3), Washington, D.C., 1969.

Poems from Black Africa, Indiana University Press, Bloomington, Indiana, 1963.

Segy, Ladislas, *African Sculpture Speaks,* Hill and Wang, 1952.

Soyinka, Wole, *Three Short Plays* (Contains "The Swamp Dwellers," "The Trials of Brother Jero," "The Strong Breed," originally published in "Five Plays." London, 1964), International University Booksellers, New York.

Smith, Godwin, *The Heritage of Man, A History of the World,* Charles Scribner's Sons, New York, 1960.

Trowell, Margaret, *African Design,* Praeger, New York, 1960.

Tucker, M., *The African in Modern Literature,* International University Booksellers, New York, 1967.

Wallbank, T. Walter and Alystair M. Taylor, *Civilization Past and Present,* 4th edition, Vol. I, Scott Foresman Co., New York, 1960.

Wingert, Paul S., *Primitive Art—Its Tradition and Style,* Meridian Books, World Publishing Co., Cleveland, 1965.

World Almanac and Book of Facts, Doubleday and Company, Inc., New York, 1968.

Worldwide Encyclopedia of Nations, "Africa," Vol. 2, ed-pub. Moske Y. Sachs, Harper and Rowe, Publishers, New York, 1967.

Slides and Film Strips.

(Association Films, Inc., 347 Madison Avenue, New York. 10017.)
  African Rhythms (1957—19 minutes, color; free loan.)
(American Library Color Slides Company, Inc., 305 East 45th Street, New York. 10017)
  MS 643—African Sculpture—University of Pennsylvania Collection. 25 color slides. Primitive representation of male and female figures, animals, etc. from various African cultures.
  24878—Benin-Queen Mother
  51667—Ife Head
  44985—Head of Benin Queen
  44981—Head of Benin Oba
  51503—Ife King
  51660—Bust of Ife King
  51504—Benin Equestrian with attendants
  51666—Benin Oba with Attendants

51665—Benin Oba with Ivory Tusk
51664—Benin Figure Holding Mace
29726—Benin Figure on Horseback
28000—Benin Head with Tusk
27999—Benin Heads with Tusks
24878—Queen Mother of Benin
28002—Benin Rooster
27998—Benin Staff Head
28012—Benin Warriors
21414—Ife Head
21411—Ife Head, Female
21405—Ife Head, Male
51675—Epa Mask—Yoruba Carving
24881—Dance Mask—Congo
44980—Two Funerary Figures—Congo.
39300—Drummer—Congo
39383—Horned Mask—Congo
43166—Mask—Congo
54377—Mask—Congo
27984—Female Fetish—Congo
27991—Baluba Dance Mask
27995—Baluba—Stool Supported by Female
27989—Bashongo Dance Mask
27986—Bateke Male Fetish
24352—Bena Lulua Mask with Beads and Cowries.
28100—Yoruba Dance Mask
28007—Yoruba Helmet Mask
28001—Yoruba Janus Faced Helmet Mask
(Arts D'Afrique Noire, Paris Ministere de la Corperation)
 N709. 6-A784-No60—Nok terra cotta; No. 59—Nok terra cotta; No. 9—Ancester Figure;
    No. 36—Janus Faced Mask; No. 88—Queen Mother of Benin; No. 85—Ife King;
    No. 86—Benin Bronze Head; No. 91—Benin Bronze Plaque; No. 90—Benin Musician
    with Flute; No. 31—Yoruba Wood Carving; No. 96—Fetish Figure; No. 42—Con-
    temporary Nigerian Wood Carver; No. 43—Contemporary Nigerian Potter.

Phono Discs:

(Folkways Scholastic Records, 50 West 44th Street, New York, N. Y. 10036.)
   FS   3854—African Music/"The Naked Prey"
   FE   4321—Music of the Jos Plateau and Other Regions of Nigeria
   FE   4338—Music of Mali
   FE   4376—Afro-Hispanic Music from Western Colombia and Equador
   FE   4402—Music of Equatorial Africa
   FE   4427—Folk Music of the Western Congo
   FE   4441—Drums of the Yoruba of Nigeria
   FE   4457—The Pygmies of the Ituri Forest
   FE   4477—The Topoke People of the Congo

FE   4502—African and Afro-American Drums
FE   4503—Africa—South of the Sahara
FE   4581—Primitive Music of the World
FW 6912—Bantu Choral Folk Songs
FC   7103—Folk Tales from West Africa

(The Record Hunter, Dept. 3-69, 507 Fifth Avenue, New York, N. Y. 10010.)
    320, C126,—*Anthologie de la vie Africaine* (Published by Ducretet-Thompson)—ethnic
    127, 128   recordings from tapes with comment in French.
    BM 30-L—*An Anthologie of African Music* (Edited by the International Music Coun-
       cil of the International Trust for Comparative Music Studies and
       Demonstration—Commentary in English, French and German—UNESCO
       Collection. The following listings may be of special interest:
       2306—Nigeria—Hausa Music
       2307—Nigeria—Hausa Music
       2303—Bezele Pygmies Music
  CLVLX296—Musique du Burundi (Congo) (Disques Vogue)
    CS8434—Olantunji and His Percussion, Brass, Woodwinds and Choir. Nigerian.
       (Columbia Records)
  FM/LP004—Aces of Highlife Music (Fisher Music, Ltd., England)

A BASIC CHART FOR THE
ANALYSIS OF ARTISTIC EXPRESSION

Content: What has been communicated?

1. What is the focus or central idea?
2. What or who has been represented? Or is it decorative, ornamental and nonrepresentational?
3. Where and/or when does it occur?
4. What is the attitude or viewpoint of the artists? Is it essentially descriptive? A protest? An advocacy? Or for entertainment and amusement?
5. Is the statement optimistic or pessimistic, happy or sad, significant or insignificant? Instructive or entertaining? Or a combination?

Technique: How has it been communicated?

1. *Medium.* What is it made of? What materials employed? (Is it poetry or prose?)
2. *Method.* How were the materials shaped or controlled? In what manner and by what means? (Devices or tools?)
3. *Pattern.* What is the sequence or order? (Chronological or otherwise?) Realistic or idealized or abstracted? In what manner was the form shaped or devised, distorted or exaggerated? Made unified?
4. *Design.* What elements of shape, form, line, color, texture?

5. *Objective*. What was the intention of the artist? What function, if any, is evident? (Include the "aesthetic.")

Evaluation: Was it worth communicating? For whom? When?

1. What is the scope? How significant? Original or imitative?
2. How well were the objectives achieved?
3. To what extent is it worth preserving Reviewing? Rereading? Rehearing?
4. Is it relevant today? Why or why not?
5. To what extent is it unique and/or universal in appeal?

Note: Some of the questions apply to several categories. Other questions might be included. Analysis should cover some of the questions from at least two of the three areas rather than attempt to answer all questions.

Index